EASY

&

DELICIOUS

PORK

RECIPES

Roberto Siciliano

INTRODUCTION

As the author of the cookbook titled **"Easy and Delicious Pork Recipes,"** I am thrilled to share with you some of my favorite pork recipes that are not only tasty but also easy to make at home.

Pork has always been a favorite meat choice for me because it is so versatile and can be used in so many different types of dishes. From savory breakfast dishes to hearty main courses and even desserts, pork can do it all! Plus, it is a great source of protein and other essential nutrients that are important for a healthy diet.

Throughout this cookbook, I have included a variety of recipes that showcase the versatility of pork. You'll find everything from classic comfort food dishes to international-inspired meals that will take your taste buds on a delicious journey.

Whether you're a beginner cook or a seasoned pro, these recipes are designed to be easy to follow and use simple ingredients that you can find at any grocery store. You'll also find plenty of helpful tips and techniques throughout the book to ensure your pork dishes turn out perfectly every time.

I hope this cookbook inspires you to get creative in the kitchen and try out some new and exciting pork recipes.

AUTHOR'S INSPIRATION

As the author of **"Easy and Delicious Pork Recipes,"** I wanted to share my passion for cooking and love for pork with others. Growing up, my family often cooked with pork, and I have always enjoyed experimenting with new recipes and cooking techniques.

Over the years, I have learned that pork is a versatile and flavorful meat that can be used in a wide range of dishes, from breakfast to dinner and everything in between. However, I also know that many people may not feel confident cooking with pork, or may be unsure of how to select the right cuts and prepare them for cooking.

This is where my inspiration for creating this cookbook comes in. I wanted to provide readers with a comprehensive guide to cooking with pork, featuring easy-to-follow recipes and practical tips for selecting, preparing, and cooking pork.

I also wanted to showcase the variety of flavors and cuisines that can be achieved with pork, from classic barbecue and Southern-style pulled pork to international dishes like Chinese-style char siu pork and German-style pork schnitzel. By sharing my favorite pork recipes, I hope to inspire readers to try new flavors and techniques in their own cooking.

Ultimately, my goal with this cookbook is to make cooking with pork accessible, enjoyable, and, most importantly, delicious. Whether you're a seasoned home cook or a novice in the kitchen, I hope that "Easy and Delicious Pork Recipes" will inspire you to get creative with pork and enjoy all that this versatile meat has to offer.

In addition to my personal inspiration for creating this cookbook, I also wanted to address a gap in the market for accessible and easy-to-follow pork recipes. While there are certainly many cookbooks and online resources available for cooking with pork, I found that many of them were geared towards experienced chefs or featured complicated techniques that could be intimidating for beginners.

I wanted to create a cookbook that would be accessible and approachable for all levels of home cooks, featuring recipes that are easy to follow and require minimal preparation and cooking time. Whether you're a busy parent looking for quick weeknight meals or a college student cooking on a budget, I believe that there is something for everyone in this cookbook.

Another aspect of my inspiration for this cookbook was the importance of eating a balanced and nutritious diet. As a nutrition enthusiast, I wanted to ensure that the recipes in this cookbook not only tasted great, but also provided a good balance of protein, healthy fats, and essential vitamins and minerals.

Whether you're looking for healthy options like grilled pork tenderloin with mango salsa or comfort food classics like pork chops with mashed potatoes and gravy, you can rest assured that the recipes in this cookbook are designed to be both delicious and nutritious.

Overall, my inspiration for creating **"Easy and Delicious Pork Recipes"** comes from a combination of my personal love for cooking with pork, a desire to make pork more accessible to home cooks, and a commitment to promoting healthy and balanced eating. I hope that this cookbook will inspire readers to get creative in the kitchen and enjoy all of the amazing flavors and possibilities that pork has to offer.

OVERVIEW

Welcome to **"Easy and Delicious Pork Recipes,"** a cookbook filled with a variety of mouth-watering and approachable recipes that are sure to satisfy any pork-lover's appetite! Whether you're a seasoned home cook or a beginner in the kitchen, this cookbook has something for everyone, with recipes ranging from breakfast dishes to main courses, sides, desserts, and more.

As someone who has always been a fan of pork, I wanted to create a cookbook that showcases the versatility and deliciousness of this protein. Pork is a meat that can be prepared in so many different ways, from crispy bacon to juicy pork chops and everything in between. I have included a range of recipes in this cookbook, so you can try out new flavors and techniques, and find your own favorite ways to cook with pork.

In addition to the recipes themselves, this cookbook includes a variety of helpful resources to guide you in the kitchen. There are tips for selecting and preparing pork, information on cooking techniques, and an ingredient and equipment glossary. There are also regional pork recipes and healthy options, so you can explore different styles of cooking and find recipes that fit your dietary needs.

I hope that this cookbook inspires you to try new things in the kitchen and to experiment with pork in all its forms. With its delicious flavors, nutritional benefits, and versatility, pork is truly a meat that can be enjoyed in so many ways. I am excited to share these recipes with you and hope that you find them as easy and delicious as I do. Enjoy!

TABLE OF CONTENTS

CHAPTER 1

Breakfast Recipes

"Easy and Delicious Pork Recipes," I wanted to include a variety of pork recipes that could be enjoyed at any meal, including breakfast. In this section of the book, I've included several mouth-watering breakfast pork recipes that are sure to become new favorites.

First up, we have Crispy Pork Belly Breakfast Sandwiches. These sandwiches are the ultimate indulgence, with crispy pork belly slices, melty cheddar cheese, and a fried egg, all sandwiched between a toasted English muffin. To make this recipe, I recommend slow-cooking the pork belly for several hours until it's tender and juicy, then crisping it up in a pan before assembling the sandwiches.

Next, we have Pork Sausage and Sweet Potato Hash, a savory and satisfying breakfast dish that's perfect for meal prep or weekend brunch. To make this recipe, you'll need ground pork sausage, sweet potatoes, onions, and a few key spices. Simply brown the sausage and sauté the sweet potatoes and onions until tender, then mix everything together for a delicious and hearty breakfast hash.

For something a little more elegant, try the Pork and Mushroom Omelette. This recipe combines tender slices of pork tenderloin with earthy mushrooms, creamy goat cheese, and fresh herbs for a delicious and filling omelette that's perfect for any occasion. To make this recipe, you'll need to cook the pork tenderloin in a skillet first, then set it aside while you sauté the mushrooms and make the omelette.

We have Slow Cooker Pork Carnitas Breakfast Tacos, a flavorful and fun twist on traditional breakfast tacos. This recipe features tender and juicy pork carnitas that are slow-cooked until they fall apart, then served in warm tortillas with scrambled eggs, avocado, salsa, and a sprinkle of fresh cilantro. To make this recipe, simply season the pork shoulder with spices and slow-cook it until it's tender and juicy, then shred it and assemble the tacos.

These breakfast pork recipes are a delicious way to start your day and add some variety to your breakfast routine. Whether you're in the mood for something indulgent like the Crispy Pork Belly Breakfast Sandwiches, or something more savory like the Pork Sausage and Sweet Potato Hash, there's a recipe in this cookbook to suit every taste and occasion.

Crispy Pork Belly Breakfast Sandwiches

This recipe combines tender and flavorful pork belly with melty cheddar cheese, a fried egg, and a toasted English muffin for a truly satisfying breakfast experience.

To start, you'll need a slab of pork belly that's been seasoned with salt and pepper and slow-cooked until it's tender and juicy. This can take several hours, but it's worth the wait to achieve the perfect texture for the pork belly. Once it's cooked, you'll need to slice it into thick pieces and crisp it up in a pan until it's golden and crispy on the outside.

While the pork belly is cooking, you can prepare the other components of the sandwich. I recommend toasting the English muffins and melting some cheddar cheese on top, and frying an egg until it's cooked to your liking.

Once all the components are ready, it's time to assemble the sandwiches. Start by placing a slice of crispy pork belly on the bottom half of the English muffin, followed by the melted cheese, the fried egg, and the top half of the English muffin. If you like, you can add some arugula or sliced tomato for some freshness and extra flavor.

The result is a truly indulgent and satisfying breakfast sandwich that's perfect for a lazy weekend brunch or a special occasion. The combination of the tender and juicy pork belly with the melty cheese and the runny egg yolk is a match made in heaven, and the toasted English muffin adds the perfect amount of crunch and texture.

The Crispy Pork Belly Breakfast Sandwiches are a must-try recipe for any pork lover looking to indulge in a delicious and hearty breakfast. The recipe is easy to follow and requires only a few key ingredients, making it a great option for a weekend morning when you have a little more time to spare in the kitchen.

Pork Sausage and Sweet Potato Hash

To make this recipe, you'll need ground pork sausage, sweet potatoes, onions, garlic, paprika, cumin, salt, and pepper. You'll also need a large skillet or cast iron pan, as well as a spatula for stirring.

To start, heat a large skillet or cast iron pan over medium-high heat. Add the ground pork sausage and cook, breaking it up into small pieces with a spatula, until it's browned and crispy, about 5-7 minutes.

Next, add the diced sweet potatoes to the skillet and sauté them with the sausage until they're tender and slightly caramelized, about 10-15 minutes. Stir in the diced onions and garlic and cook for another 2-3 minutes, until the onions are translucent and fragrant.

To season the hash, I like to use a blend of paprika, cumin, salt, and pepper, which adds a smoky and slightly spicy flavor to the dish. You can adjust the seasoning to your liking, adding more or less of each spice as desired.

Once the hash is fully cooked and seasoned, you can serve it as is, or top it with a fried egg for an extra protein boost. The sweet and savory flavors of the sweet potatoes and pork sausage make this dish incredibly satisfying and filling, while the blend of spices adds depth and complexity to the flavor profile.

The Pork Sausage and Sweet Potato Hash recipe in my cookbook is an easy and delicious way to incorporate more pork into your breakfast routine. It's a great option for meal prep, as the leftovers can be stored in the fridge and reheated throughout the week for a quick and easy breakfast option.

Pork and Mushroom Omelette

To make this omelette, you'll need the following ingredients:

2 tablespoons of butter
1/2 cup of sliced mushrooms
2 cloves of minced garlic
1/4 teaspoon of dried thyme
4 large eggs
1/4 cup of milk
1/2 cup of cooked and sliced pork tenderloin
1/4 cup of crumbled goat cheese
Salt and black pepper to taste

Fresh chopped herbs (such as parsley or chives) for garnish
To begin, heat a non-stick skillet over medium-high heat and add the butter. Once the butter has melted, add the sliced mushrooms and sauté them for about 5 minutes until they are soft and tender. Next, add the minced garlic and dried thyme and cook for an additional minute until fragrant.

In a separate bowl, whisk together the eggs and milk until well-combined. Season with salt and black pepper to taste. Pour the egg mixture into the skillet with the mushrooms and let it cook for about 2-3 minutes until the eggs begin to set.

Once the eggs are set, add the cooked and sliced pork tenderloin to one half of the omelette, and sprinkle the crumbled goat cheese on top. Use a spatula to gently fold the other half of the omelette over the filling, creating a half-moon shape. Let the omelette cook for another minute or so until the cheese is melted and the eggs are fully cooked.

To serve, slide the omelette onto a plate and garnish with fresh chopped herbs. This Pork and Mushroom Omelette is a delicious and hearty breakfast option that's perfect for any occasion. The tender pork, earthy mushrooms, and creamy goat cheese all come together to create a flavorful and satisfying dish that's sure to become a new favorite.

Slow Cooker Pork Carnitas Breakfast Tacos

This flavorful and fun twist on traditional breakfast tacos is perfect for a weekend brunch or a quick and easy weekday breakfast.

To start, you'll need a few key ingredients: a pork shoulder roast, onion, garlic, orange juice, lime juice, chili powder, cumin, oregano, and salt. You'll also need some toppings to garnish the tacos, such as scrambled eggs, diced avocado, salsa, and fresh cilantro.

To make the pork carnitas, simply season the pork shoulder with the spices and place it in a slow cooker along with the chopped onion, garlic, orange juice, and lime juice. Cover the slow cooker and cook on low for 8-10 hours, until the pork is tender and falls apart easily.

Once the pork is done cooking, remove it from the slow cooker and shred it using two forks. Then, return the shredded pork to the slow cooker and cook on high for an additional 30 minutes to allow the flavors to meld together.

To assemble the breakfast tacos, warm up some corn tortillas in a skillet and fill them with scrambled eggs, the shredded pork carnitas, diced avocado, salsa, and a sprinkle of fresh cilantro. Serve hot and enjoy!

This recipe is not only delicious, but it's also easy to customize to suit your tastes. You can add or subtract spices to make it more or less spicy, or swap out toppings to make it your own. Plus, because it's made in a slow cooker, it's easy to prepare in advance and have ready for a quick and easy breakfast on a busy weekday morning.

This Slow Cooker Pork Carnitas Breakfast Tacos recipe is a delicious and fun way to switch up your breakfast routine and add some variety to your meals.

CHAPTER 2

Appetizers and Snacks

In this section of the book, I've included several mouth-watering and easy-to-make pork appetizers and snacks that are sure to impress your guests or satisfy your hunger.

First up, we have Bacon-Wrapped Dates, a sweet and savory appetizer that's always a crowd-pleaser. To make this recipe, you'll need pitted dates, bacon, and toothpicks. Simply wrap each date with a slice of bacon, secure with a toothpick, and bake until the bacon is crispy and the dates are warmed through. This is an easy and delicious appetizer that can be prepared in advance and served at room temperature.

Next, we have Pork and Cheddar Cheese Dip, a cheesy and creamy dip that's perfect for snacking or entertaining. To make this recipe, you'll need ground pork, cheddar cheese, cream cheese, sour cream, and a few key spices. Simply brown the pork in a skillet, mix it with the cheeses and spices, and bake until the dip is hot and bubbly. Serve with your favorite crackers or chips for an irresistible snack.

For something a little more substantial, try the Pork and Pineapple Skewers. This recipe features juicy pork tenderloin, sweet pineapple chunks, and a flavorful marinade that's perfect for grilling or broiling. To make this recipe, simply marinate the pork and pineapple in the marinade for a few hours, then skewer them and grill or broil until they're tender and charred. This is a fun and flavorful appetizer that's sure to impress your guests.

We have Bacon-Wrapped Jalapeno Poppers, a spicy and cheesy appetizer that's perfect for game day or any gathering. To make this recipe, you'll need jalapeno peppers, cream cheese, shredded cheddar cheese, and bacon. Simply stuff each jalapeno half with the cheese mixture, wrap with a slice of bacon, and bake until the bacon is crispy and the peppers are tender. This is a delicious and addictive appetizer that's always a hit.

These pork appetizers and snacks are easy to make, delicious, and sure to satisfy your hunger. Whether you're in the mood for something sweet and savory like the Bacon-Wrapped Dates, or something spicy and cheesy like the Bacon-Wrapped Jalapeno Poppers, there's a recipe in this cookbook to suit every taste and occasion.

Bacon Wrapped Dates

Bacon Wrapped Dates are a delicious and easy-to-make appetizer that is sure to impress your guests. As the author of the cookbook titled "Easy and Delicious Pork Recipes," I wanted to include this recipe because it's a crowd-pleaser that requires minimal ingredients and preparation.

To make Bacon Wrapped Dates, you'll need just three ingredients: pitted dates, bacon, and toothpicks. Start by preheating your oven to 400°F and lining a baking sheet with parchment paper. Take each date and wrap it tightly with a strip of bacon, then secure it with a toothpick. Repeat this process with the remaining dates until all are wrapped in bacon.

Next, place the bacon-wrapped dates on the prepared baking sheet and bake in the oven for 15-20 minutes, or until the bacon is crispy and golden brown. Once the Bacon Wrapped Dates are cooked, remove them from the oven and allow them to cool for a few minutes before serving.

Bacon Wrapped Dates can be served as a sweet and salty appetizer that is perfect for entertaining. The sweetness of the dates pairs perfectly with the salty and smoky flavor of the bacon, making it a winning combination. This recipe is also very versatile, and you can easily experiment with different types of bacon or adding in some spices or herbs to the mix.

Additionally, Bacon Wrapped Dates can be made ahead of time and reheated in the oven just before serving, which makes them an excellent option for parties or gatherings. They're also perfect for game day or movie night snacks!

Bacon Wrapped Dates are a simple yet elegant appetizer that is sure to impress your guests. They're easy to make, packed with flavor, and perfect for any occasion. This recipe is a must-try for anyone looking to add some variety and excitement to their appetizer repertoire.

Sticky Soy and Honey Pork Bites

This dish is a perfect balance of sweet and savory flavors and is a crowd-pleaser for any occasion, from a weeknight dinner to a party appetizer.

To make this recipe, you'll need pork tenderloin, soy sauce, honey, garlic, ginger, green onions, and sesame seeds. Begin by cutting the pork tenderloin into bite-sized pieces and marinating it in a mixture of soy sauce, honey, minced garlic, and grated ginger. Let the pork marinate for at least 30 minutes or up to overnight to allow the flavors to develop.

Once the pork has marinated, heat a large skillet over medium-high heat and add the pork pieces. Cook the pork until it is browned on all sides and cooked through, about 5-7 minutes. Then, add the remaining marinade to the skillet and cook for an additional 2-3 minutes, until the sauce has thickened and coated the pork pieces.

To finish the dish, sprinkle the cooked pork bites with sliced green onions and sesame seeds. The result is a deliciously sticky and flavorful dish that's sure to be a hit with everyone at the table.

One of the things I love about this recipe is how versatile it is. You can serve the pork bites as an appetizer, either on their own or with toothpicks for easy eating. They also make a great main course when served with rice and vegetables. Leftovers can be stored in the fridge for a few days and reheated for an easy and delicious meal.

These Sticky Soy and Honey Pork Bites are a great addition to any meal plan, providing a sweet and savory protein option that's easy to prepare and sure to impress. I hope you enjoy this recipe as much as I do!

Pork Rind Nachos

Nachos - a fun and flavorful twist on traditional nachos.
To start, you'll need a bag of high-quality pork rinds. Choose a brand that's thick and sturdy, so that the rinds can hold up to the weight of the toppings. Spread the pork rinds out on a baking sheet lined with parchment paper, and sprinkle with a generous amount of shredded cheese. I recommend using a blend of sharp cheddar and Monterey Jack cheese for a perfect balance of flavor.

Next, it's time to add the toppings. You can customize your Pork Rind Nachos with any toppings you like, but some of my favorites include crumbled cooked sausage, diced tomatoes, sliced jalapeños, and sliced black olives. You could also add some chopped cilantro, sliced scallions, or a dollop of sour cream for even more flavor.

Once you've added all of your desired toppings, pop the baking sheet into the oven and bake at 350°F for 10-12 minutes, or until the cheese is melted and bubbly. Be careful not to over-bake the pork rinds, as they can become too crunchy and lose their texture.

When the Pork Rind Nachos are finished baking, remove the baking sheet from the oven and let it cool for a few minutes. Then, use a spatula to carefully transfer the nachos to a serving platter, being sure to keep the toppings intact.

Serve the Pork Rind Nachos hot, with additional toppings on the side if desired. This snack is perfect for game day, movie night, or any time you're craving something salty and satisfying.

This recipe for Pork Rind Nachos is a fun and easy way to enjoy the crunch of traditional nachos, with the added protein and flavor of crispy pork rinds. It's a perfect recipe for anyone looking for a low-carb or gluten-free snack option that's still delicious and satisfying.

Crispy Pork Belly Bites with Garlic Aioli

This recipe is the perfect appetizer or party snack, with crispy and flavorful bites of pork belly served alongside a creamy garlic aioli dipping sauce.

To make this recipe, you'll need a few key ingredients, including pork belly, salt, black pepper, garlic powder, and olive oil. Start by cutting the pork belly into bite-sized pieces and seasoning them with salt, pepper, and garlic powder. Then, heat some olive oil in a skillet over medium-high heat and add the pork belly pieces, cooking them for several minutes on each side until they're crispy and golden brown.

Once the pork belly bites are cooked to perfection, it's time to make the garlic aioli dipping sauce. This is a simple and flavorful sauce that's made with mayonnaise, minced garlic, lemon juice, and salt. Simply whisk everything together until it's smooth and creamy, then serve alongside the crispy pork belly bites.

What I love about this recipe is that it's both indulgent and easy to make. The pork belly is incredibly flavorful and crispy, with just the right amount of salt and garlic seasoning. And the garlic aioli dipping sauce is the perfect complement, adding a creamy and tangy flavor that perfectly balances the richness of the pork.

I recommend serving these Crispy Pork Belly Bites with Garlic Aioli as an appetizer at your next party or gathering, or even as a fun and unexpected snack for a movie night at home. They're sure to be a hit with pork lovers and anyone who enjoys a tasty and satisfying appetizer.

This recipe is a delicious and easy way to enjoy the rich flavor and texture of pork belly in a fun and approachable way. So why not give it a try and see for yourself how delicious it can be

CHAPTER 3

Pan-Seared Pork Chops with Apples and Onions

This recipe combines tender pork chops with sweet and savory flavors for a mouth-watering main course that's perfect for a cozy dinner at home.

To start, you'll need bone-in pork chops, which are more flavorful and tender than boneless chops. Season them with salt, pepper, and a few spices like paprika or garlic powder. Then, heat some oil in a large skillet over medium-high heat and add the pork chops. Cook them for about 4-5 minutes per side, until they're browned and cooked through.

Next, add sliced apples and onions to the skillet and cook them until they're soft and caramelized. The apples add a touch of sweetness to the dish, while the onions add a savory depth of flavor. You can also add a splash of apple cider vinegar to the skillet to deglaze it and create a delicious sauce.

Finally, garnish the dish with some fresh herbs like thyme or parsley, and serve the pork chops with the apple and onion mixture on top. You can also serve it with a side of roasted vegetables or a simple salad.

This dish is perfect for a cozy fall or winter dinner, and it's also great for entertaining. The combination of tender pork chops with sweet and savory flavors is sure to impress your guests. Plus, it's easy to make and requires just a few ingredients.

Pan-Seared Pork Chops with Apples and Onions is a delicious and easy recipe that's perfect for any occasion. It's a great way to elevate a simple pork chop into a flavorful and satisfying meal.

Slow Cooker Pulled Pork Sandwiches

This recipe is not only easy to prepare, but it's also packed with flavor and perfect for feeding a crowd.

To make this recipe, you'll need a pork shoulder or pork butt, which are both great cuts of meat for slow cooking. First, you'll want to season the pork with a blend of spices, such as paprika, garlic powder, onion powder, and chili powder, to give it plenty of flavor. Then, simply place the pork in a slow cooker along with some onions, garlic, and a bit of chicken broth or apple cider vinegar to keep it moist.

The pork will need to cook on low heat for several hours until it's fall-apart tender. I recommend cooking it for at least 8 hours, but you can also cook it overnight or for up to 10 hours for even more flavor and tenderness. Once the pork is done cooking, you'll want to remove it from the slow cooker and shred it with a fork.

To assemble the sandwiches, simply pile the shredded pork onto a soft bun or roll, and top it with your favorite barbecue sauce or other condiments, such as coleslaw, pickles, or cheese. I like to serve these sandwiches with a side of baked beans or potato salad for a classic barbecue meal.

One of the great things about this recipe is that it's easy to customize to your tastes. You can adjust the spice level of the seasoning blend or experiment with different barbecue sauces or toppings to make it your own. Plus, the leftovers can be used in a variety of ways, such as in tacos, burritos, or even on pizza.

Slow Cooker Pulled Pork Sandwiches are a classic and delicious way to enjoy pork. With just a few simple ingredients and some time in the slow cooker, you can create a mouth-watering meal that's perfect for any occasion.

Garlic and Herb Roasted Pork Tenderloin

This recipe is a perfect example of how easy it can be to create a delicious and flavorful pork dish with just a few simple ingredients.

To make this recipe, you'll need a pork tenderloin, garlic, fresh herbs (such as rosemary, thyme, and oregano), salt, pepper, and olive oil. Start by preheating your oven to 400°F (200°C) and lining a baking dish with parchment paper. Then, pat the pork tenderloin dry with paper towels and place it in the baking dish.

Next, mince the garlic and chop the fresh herbs, then mix them together with some salt, pepper, and olive oil to make a fragrant herb paste. Rub the herb paste all over the pork tenderloin, making sure to coat it evenly on all sides.

Roast the pork tenderloin in the oven for about 20-25 minutes, or until the internal temperature reaches 145°F (63°C) when measured with a meat thermometer. Let the pork rest for a few minutes before slicing and serving.

The result is a tender and juicy pork tenderloin that's bursting with flavor from the garlic and herbs. This recipe is perfect for a simple weeknight dinner, but it's also elegant enough to serve to guests for a dinner party or holiday meal.

To switch things up, you could also try adding other flavorings to the herb paste, such as lemon zest, Dijon mustard, or honey. You could also serve the pork with a side of roasted vegetables or a simple green salad for a complete and satisfying meal.

Garlic and Herb Roasted Pork Tenderloin recipe is a delicious and easy way to enjoy pork at home. With just a few simple ingredients and a little bit of time in the oven, you can create a meal that's sure to impress.

Pork and Vegetable Stir Fry

This Pork and Vegetable Stir Fry is a great way to incorporate more veggies into your diet while also enjoying the bold flavors of pork and Asian spices.

To start, you'll need to gather your ingredients. For this recipe, you'll need thinly sliced pork tenderloin, a variety of colorful vegetables like bell peppers, broccoli florets, and snow peas, garlic, ginger, soy sauce, sesame oil, and a few other pantry staples.

To make the stir fry, you'll start by heating some oil in a wok or large skillet over high heat. Once the oil is hot, add the pork and stir-fry it until it's browned and crispy. Remove the pork from the skillet and set it aside.

Next, add the vegetables to the skillet and stir-fry them until they're tender-crisp. Then, add the garlic and ginger and cook for another minute or so until fragrant. Finally, add the pork back to the skillet, along with the soy sauce, sesame oil, and any other seasonings you like. Toss everything together until well-coated and heated through, then serve over steamed rice or noodles.

This Pork and Vegetable Stir Fry is not only delicious, but it's also packed with nutrients from the colorful array of vegetables. The pork adds a satisfying protein boost, while the Asian-inspired flavors of garlic, ginger, and soy sauce give the dish a bold and satisfying flavor profile. Plus, it's easy to customize based on your preferences or what you have on hand. For example, you could swap in different veggies, like bok choy, mushrooms, or zucchini, or adjust the seasonings to your liking.

This Pork and Vegetable Stir Fry is a healthy, flavorful, and easy-to-make recipe that's perfect for busy weeknights or anytime you're in the mood for a satisfying Asian-inspired dish.

Instant Pot Pork Ramen

This recipe is perfect for a quick and satisfying dinner, and the Instant Pot makes it a breeze to cook the pork to tender perfection.

To start, you'll need a few key ingredients, including pork shoulder or butt, fresh ginger, garlic, soy sauce, mirin, and chicken broth. You'll also need some dried ramen noodles, which can be found in the international section of most grocery stores.

To begin, I recommend cutting the pork shoulder into large chunks and seasoning it with salt and pepper. Then, using the Instant Pot's sauté function, brown the pork on all sides until it's golden brown and crispy. Remove the pork from the pot and set it aside while you prepare the broth.

To make the broth, sauté the ginger and garlic in the Instant Pot until fragrant, then add the soy sauce, mirin, and chicken broth. Return the pork to the pot, making sure it's submerged in the broth, and set the Instant Pot to cook on high pressure for 60 minutes. Once the cooking time is up, allow the pressure to release naturally for 10 minutes before manually releasing any remaining pressure.

While the pork is cooking, prepare the ramen noodles according to the package instructions. Once the pork is done cooking, remove it from the Instant Pot and shred it with two forks. To assemble the ramen bowls, add the cooked noodles to a bowl and top with the shredded pork, broth, and any desired toppings such as soft-boiled eggs, sliced green onions, and sliced mushrooms.

This Instant Pot Pork Ramen recipe is a delicious and easy way to enjoy a classic Japanese dish in the comfort of your own home. The tender pork and flavorful broth are sure to satisfy any cravings for a warm and comforting meal, and the Instant Pot makes it a breeze to prepare. To make this recipe even easier, you can prepare the pork ahead of time and store it in the fridge or freezer until you're ready to make the ramen. You can also customize the toppings to suit your tastes – some other great options include sliced bamboo shoots, corn, nori, and sesame seeds.

Another great thing about this recipe is that it's easy to adapt to your dietary preferences. If you're looking for a lower-carb option, you can substitute the ramen noodles for zucchini noodles or shirataki noodles. And if you're looking for a gluten-free option, be sure to use gluten-free soy sauce and check that your chicken broth is gluten-free as well. This Instant Pot Pork Ramen recipe is a delicious and easy way to enjoy a classic Japanese dish in the comfort of your own home. Whether you're new to cooking with an Instant Pot or a seasoned pro, this recipe is sure to become a new favorite in your meal rotation.

Slow Cooker BBQ Ribs

I am excited to share with you one of my favorite pork recipes - Slow Cooker BBQ Ribs. This recipe is perfect for those days when you want something flavorful and satisfying, but don't want to spend all day in the kitchen.

To start, you'll need a few key ingredients: pork ribs, your favorite BBQ sauce, and some seasonings. I recommend using baby back ribs for this recipe, as they're a bit smaller and cook more quickly than spare ribs. You'll also need to season the ribs with a dry rub of brown sugar, paprika, garlic powder, onion powder, and salt.

Once your ribs are seasoned, it's time to start cooking. The beauty of this recipe is that it's done in a slow cooker, so you can set it and forget it until it's time to eat. Simply place the seasoned ribs in the slow cooker and pour the BBQ sauce over them, making sure to coat the ribs evenly. Then, cover the slow cooker and cook on low for 6-8 hours, until the ribs are tender and falling off the bone.

When the ribs are done cooking, remove them from the slow cooker and place them on a baking sheet. Brush them with additional BBQ sauce, if desired, and place them under the broiler for a few minutes to caramelize and get a bit of char.

Serve your Slow Cooker BBQ Ribs with your favorite sides, like coleslaw, baked beans, or corn on the cob. This recipe is perfect for a family dinner, backyard BBQ, or any time you're craving some delicious and easy-to-make pork ribs.

This Slow Cooker BBQ Ribs recipe is a great addition to any pork lover's recipe collection. It's easy to make, full of flavor, and perfect for those days when you want something comforting and satisfying without a lot of fuss. I hope you enjoy making and eating this recipe as much as I do!

CHAPTER 4

Side Dishes

I know that a great side dish can really take a pork recipe to the next level. That's why I've included a variety of tasty and easy-to-make side dish recipes that pair perfectly with pork.

First up, we have Garlic Roasted Green Beans. This simple side dish features tender green beans tossed in garlic and olive oil, then roasted until they're crisp-tender and slightly caramelized. It's a quick and easy recipe that's perfect for busy weeknights or holiday meals.

Another delicious side dish to serve with pork is Sweet Potato and Apple Casserole. This hearty and comforting dish combines sweet potatoes, apples, and a sweet, cinnamon-sugar topping for a crowd-pleasing side that's perfect for fall or winter. To make this recipe, simply layer thinly sliced sweet potatoes and apples in a baking dish, then sprinkle with a mixture of brown sugar, cinnamon, and butter before baking.

For something a little lighter, try the Summer Corn Salad with Bacon and Avocado. This colorful salad is packed with fresh corn, crispy bacon, creamy avocado, and a tangy lime dressing, making it the perfect side dish for summer barbecues or picnics. To make this recipe, simply sauté the corn and bacon in a pan, then toss with diced avocado, cherry tomatoes, and a simple lime vinaigrette.

We have Roasted Brussels Sprouts with Bacon and Balsamic. This savory and satisfying side dish features crispy roasted Brussels sprouts tossed with salty bacon and tangy balsamic vinegar for a flavor-packed side that's perfect for any pork recipe. To make this recipe, simply roast the Brussels sprouts until tender and caramelized, then toss with crispy bacon and a drizzle of balsamic vinegar.

These side dish recipes are a great way to elevate your pork dishes and add some variety to your meal planning. Whether you're in the mood for something savory like the Roasted Brussels Sprouts with Bacon and Balsamic, or something sweet like the Sweet Potato and Apple Casserole, there's a recipe in this cookbook to suit every taste and occasion.

Garlic Parmesan Roasted Potatoes with Bacon

This recipe is perfect as a side dish for pork dishes or as a stand-alone dish for a tasty lunch or dinner.

To start, you'll need to gather your ingredients: 2 pounds of baby potatoes, 4-6 slices of bacon, 2 tablespoons of olive oil, 2 cloves of minced garlic, 1/4 cup of grated Parmesan cheese, salt, and pepper.

Begin by preheating your oven to 400°F. Next, wash and dry the baby potatoes, then cut them in half. Place the halved potatoes in a large bowl and drizzle them with olive oil. Sprinkle the minced garlic, salt, and pepper over the potatoes and toss them to coat evenly.

Next, lay the bacon slices out on a baking sheet lined with parchment paper. Place the baking sheet in the preheated oven and cook the bacon for 10-12 minutes, or until it's crispy. Remove the bacon from the oven and let it cool for a few minutes before crumbling it into small pieces.

Now, add the crumbled bacon to the bowl of seasoned potatoes and toss them together. Spread the potatoes and bacon out on a baking sheet in a single layer and roast them in the preheated oven for 20-25 minutes, or until the potatoes are tender and golden brown.

Once the potatoes are done roasting, remove them from the oven and sprinkle them with grated Parmesan cheese. Toss the potatoes gently to coat them with the cheese, then transfer them to a serving dish and enjoy!

These Garlic Parmesan Roasted Potatoes with Bacon are a delicious and easy-to-prepare side dish that pairs perfectly with any pork recipe. The combination of tender baby potatoes, crispy bacon, and savory Parmesan cheese makes this dish both satisfying and flavorful.

One of the great things about this recipe is how customizable it is. You can adjust the seasoning and the amount of bacon or Parmesan cheese to your liking, or even add other herbs and spices to the mix.

For example, you could add some chopped fresh rosemary or thyme to the potatoes for an extra burst of flavor, or sprinkle some red pepper flakes over the finished dish for a little bit of heat.

Another variation you could try is using different types of potatoes. While baby potatoes work well in this recipe, you could also use larger potatoes that have been chopped into smaller pieces. Red potatoes or Yukon Gold potatoes would both work well.

If you're looking for a vegetarian option, you could omit the bacon and add some roasted or sautéed vegetables instead. Bell peppers, zucchini, or mushrooms would all be delicious additions.

Garlic Parmesan Roasted Potatoes with Bacon recipe is a versatile and tasty side dish that's sure to become a family favorite. Whether you're serving it with pork chops, roast pork, or another pork dish from this cookbook, these potatoes will add a delicious and satisfying element to your meal.

Creamy Polenta with Crispy Pork Belly

To make this recipe, you'll need to start by slow-cooking the pork belly in the oven until it's tender and juicy. This can take several hours, but the end result is worth the wait - the pork belly will be melt-in-your-mouth tender, with a crispy exterior that adds the perfect amount of texture.

While the pork belly is cooking, you can prepare the creamy polenta. Polenta is a simple and hearty dish made from cornmeal, water, and a little bit of butter or cream. To make the creamy polenta for this recipe, simply whisk together the cornmeal and water in a saucepan, then cook over low heat until it thickens into a creamy, porridge-like consistency. Once the polenta is cooked, you can stir in some butter or cream for added richness and flavor.

To assemble the dish, simply spoon the creamy polenta onto a plate and top it with a few slices of the crispy pork belly. You can also add some sautéed greens or roasted vegetables on the side for a balanced and satisfying meal.

The result is a dish that's creamy, savory, and oh-so-indulgent. The creamy polenta provides a perfect base for the crispy pork belly, which adds a rich and savory flavor to every bite. This dish is perfect for a cozy weeknight dinner, a special occasion, or even a brunch dish that's sure to impress your guests.

This Creamy Polenta with Crispy Pork Belly recipe is a delicious and easy way to showcase the versatility and flavor of pork belly, while also highlighting the comforting and satisfying nature of polenta. It's a must-try recipe for any pork lover looking for a new and delicious way to enjoy this delicious meat.

Roasted Brussels Sprouts with Bacon

This dish is a perfect accompaniment to any pork main dish and is easy to prepare with just a few simple ingredients.

To start, you'll need to preheat your oven to 400°F (200°C). Next, trim the ends off of one pound of Brussels sprouts and slice them in half lengthwise. Spread them out on a baking sheet and drizzle with olive oil, salt, and pepper. Then, add 6-8 slices of bacon to the baking sheet, either chopped or whole.

Roast the Brussels sprouts and bacon in the oven for 20-25 minutes or until the sprouts are tender and the bacon is crispy. While the sprouts and bacon are roasting, prepare the garlic-balsamic glaze. Mince 3 cloves of garlic and add them to a small saucepan with 1/4 cup of balsamic vinegar, 1 tablespoon of honey, and a pinch of red pepper flakes. Heat the glaze over medium-high heat, stirring occasionally, until it has thickened and reduced by half.

Once the Brussels sprouts and bacon are done roasting, remove them from the oven and drizzle the garlic-balsamic glaze over the top. Use tongs to toss everything together until the sprouts and bacon are coated in the glaze.

This Roasted Brussels Sprouts with Bacon recipe is the perfect combination of sweet and savory flavors, with the bacon adding a smoky, salty flavor that complements the sweetness of the balsamic glaze. Plus, the Brussels sprouts are a healthy and nutritious addition to any meal. This dish is easy to customize too - you can add additional seasonings like garlic powder or rosemary to the sprouts or use a different type of vinegar in the glaze, like apple cider or red wine vinegar.

This Roasted Brussels Sprouts with Bacon recipe is a simple but delicious side dish that's perfect for any meal featuring pork. Not only is this dish a great side for pork, but it's also a fantastic addition to any holiday or special occasion meal. The colors of the Brussels sprouts and bacon add a beautiful pop of green and brown to the table, making it a visually appealing dish.

One of the best things about this recipe is its versatility. It can be served warm or at room temperature, making it a great option for potlucks or holiday gatherings where you need a dish that can be served at any temperature. Plus, it's easy to double or triple the recipe if you're feeding a crowd.

If you're looking to make this recipe even healthier, you can use turkey bacon instead of regular bacon or omit the bacon altogether for a vegetarian version. The garlic-balsamic glaze is also a great addition to other roasted vegetables like carrots or sweet potatoes, so feel free to experiment and find your favorite combinations.

Roasted Brussels Sprouts with Bacon is a simple but flavorful side dish that's perfect for any meal featuring pork. The combination of roasted Brussels sprouts and crispy bacon, coated in a sweet and tangy garlic-balsamic glaze, is sure to be a hit with any crowd. So, give this recipe a try and enjoy a delicious and easy-to-make side dish that's packed with flavor!

Fried Rice with Pork and Vegetables

I'm excited to share one of my favorite pork recipes with you: Fried Rice with Pork and Vegetables.

This dish is a classic Chinese takeout favorite that's easy to make at home and can be customized to your liking with your favorite vegetables and seasonings. Here's how to make it:

Ingredients:

3 cups cooked white rice, chilled
1/2 lb. pork tenderloin, sliced into thin strips
1 cup mixed vegetables (such as carrots, peas, corn, and green beans), diced
2 cloves garlic, minced
2 eggs, beaten
2 tablespoons soy sauce
1 tablespoon oyster sauce
1 tablespoon sesame oil
Salt and pepper, to taste
Green onions and sesame seeds, for garnish

Instructions:

- Heat a large wok or skillet over high heat. Add a tablespoon of oil and swirl to coat the pan.
- Add the sliced pork and stir-fry until browned and cooked through, about 3-4 minutes. Remove from the pan and set aside.

- In the same pan, add another tablespoon of oil and sauté the garlic and vegetables until tender, about 3-4 minutes.
- Push the vegetables to the sides of the pan and pour the beaten eggs into the center. Scramble the eggs until they're cooked through, then stir them into the vegetables.
- Add the chilled rice to the pan and stir-fry until heated through and lightly browned, about 5-6 minutes.
- Add the cooked pork back into the pan and stir to combine.
- In a small bowl, whisk together the soy sauce, oyster sauce, sesame oil, salt, and pepper. Pour the sauce over the fried rice and stir to coat.
- Garnish with chopped green onions and sesame seeds before serving.

This Fried Rice with Pork and Vegetables recipe is a great way to use up leftover rice and make a satisfying and flavorful meal in no time. The combination of tender pork, mixed vegetables, and fluffy rice makes for a filling and nutritious meal that's perfect for lunch or dinner. Plus, with just a few pantry staples and some fresh ingredients, you can make this dish at home for a fraction of the cost of takeout. Enjoy!

Loaded Baked Sweet Potatoes with Pulled Pork

Loaded Baked Sweet Potatoes with Pulled Pork is one of my favorite recipes in this cookbook. This dish is a perfect combination of sweet and savory, with tender pulled pork and baked sweet potatoes topped with a variety of flavorful toppings.

To make this recipe, start by baking sweet potatoes in the oven until they're soft and tender. While the sweet potatoes are baking, prepare the pulled pork. You can use leftover pulled pork or make a fresh batch using a slow cooker or pressure cooker. Once the pulled pork is ready, set it aside and prepare the toppings.

For this recipe, I recommend topping the sweet potatoes with a mixture of tangy barbecue sauce, creamy avocado, and sharp cheddar cheese. You can also add other toppings like diced tomatoes, green onions, and jalapenos to give the dish an extra kick of flavor.

To assemble the dish, simply slice open the baked sweet potatoes and fill them with a generous helping of pulled pork. Drizzle with barbecue sauce and top with the avocado and cheese mixture. Bake the sweet potatoes in the oven for a few more minutes until the cheese is melted and bubbly, then add any additional toppings you desire.

Loaded Baked Sweet Potatoes with Pulled Pork is a versatile recipe that can be enjoyed as a main dish or as a side dish. It's perfect for a cozy family dinner or a casual gathering with friends. Plus, it's easy to customize to your liking by adding or removing toppings based on your preferences.

This recipe is a delicious and satisfying way to enjoy pork and sweet potatoes in a unique and flavorful way. Give it a try and see why it's one of my favorites!
One of the things I love about this recipe is that it's also a great way to use up any leftover pulled pork you might have from a previous meal. You can easily make a big batch of pulled pork and use it for multiple meals throughout the week, including this recipe.

Another great thing about this dish is that it's incredibly nutritious. Sweet potatoes are packed with vitamins and minerals, including vitamin A, potassium, and fiber. They're also a great source of complex carbohydrates, which provide sustained energy throughout the day. The pulled pork is also a great source of protein, which is important for building and repairing muscle tissue.

To make this recipe even healthier, you can use low-sugar or sugar-free barbecue sauce and opt for reduced-fat cheese. You can also use a lean cut of pork for the pulled pork, such as pork loin or tenderloin.

Loaded Baked Sweet Potatoes with Pulled Pork is a delicious and healthy recipe that's perfect for any occasion. Whether you're looking for a quick and easy dinner or a dish to impress your guests, this recipe is sure to satisfy you.

CHAPTER 5

Sauces and Marinades

I believe that sauces and marinades are essential components of any great pork recipe. In this section of the book, I'll be sharing some of my favorite pork marinades and sauces that will elevate any pork dish to the next level.

First, let's talk marinades. A good marinade can infuse pork with flavor and make it tender and juicy. One of my go-to marinades is a simple combination of soy sauce, brown sugar, garlic, and ginger. This marinade is perfect for Asian-inspired dishes like stir-fries, grilled pork chops, or pork kebabs. To make it, simply whisk together the ingredients and marinate the pork for at least 30 minutes before cooking.

Another delicious marinade is a combination of balsamic vinegar, honey, and Dijon mustard. This sweet and tangy marinade is perfect for pork tenderloin or pork chops, and it's easy to make with ingredients you probably already have in your pantry.

Now, let's move on to sauces. A good sauce can take a pork dish from ordinary to extraordinary. One of my favorite pork sauces is a classic barbecue sauce. I like to make my own with ketchup, brown sugar, apple cider vinegar, Worcestershire sauce, and a few spices. This sauce is perfect for pulled pork sandwiches, grilled ribs, or any other barbecue-inspired pork dish.

Another delicious sauce for pork is a creamy mustard sauce. This sauce is made with Dijon mustard, sour cream, and a few other ingredients. It's perfect for serving with pork tenderloin or pork chops and adds a tangy and creamy element to any pork dish.

Finally, let's not forget about gravy. Pork gravy is the perfect finishing touch for pork chops or roasted pork loin. To make a delicious pork gravy, start by making a roux with butter and flour, then whisk in chicken broth, milk, and pork drippings. Simmer until thickened, and season with salt and pepper to taste.

These sauces and marinades are essential components of any great pork recipe. Whether you're in the mood for an Asian-inspired marinade, a classic barbecue sauce, or a creamy mustard sauce, there's a sauce or marinade in this cookbook to suit every taste and occasion.

Tangy BBQ Sauce

This BBQ sauce is a great addition to any grilled or roasted pork dish, and it's easy to make with just a few simple ingredients.

To make this Tangy BBQ Sauce, you'll need the following ingredients:

1 cup ketchup
1/2 cup apple cider vinegar
1/4 cup molasses
1/4 cup brown sugar
1 tablespoon Worcestershire sauce
1 teaspoon smoked paprika
1/2 teaspoon garlic powder
1/2 teaspoon onion powder
1/2 teaspoon salt
1/4 teaspoon black pepper

To prepare the sauce, simply combine all of the ingredients in a saucepan over medium heat. Bring the mixture to a simmer, stirring occasionally, and let it cook for 5-10 minutes until it's thickened and all of the flavors have melded together.

The key to the tangy flavor of this BBQ sauce is the combination of apple cider vinegar, molasses, and brown sugar. The apple cider vinegar adds a bright and tangy flavor to the sauce, while the molasses and brown sugar give it a sweet and slightly smoky flavor. The smoked paprika, garlic powder, onion powder, salt, and pepper add depth and complexity to the sauce.

Once you've made the Tangy BBQ Sauce, you can use it to marinate pork chops or ribs, baste a pork roast while it's cooking, or simply serve it as a dipping sauce on the side. It's a versatile sauce that pairs well with a variety of pork dishes, from grilled pork tenderloin to slow-cooked pulled pork.

This Tangy BBQ Sauce is a must-have recipe for any pork lover. It's easy to make, flavorful, and adds a delicious tangy sweetness to any pork dish. Give it a try and see how it takes your pork dishes to the next level.

Sweet and Spicy Soy Glaze

I developed this Sweet and Spicy Soy Glaze, which is perfect for adding a bold and delicious flavor to everything from pork chops to pork tenderloin.

To make the glaze, you'll need a few key ingredients, including soy sauce, honey, garlic, chili flakes, and sesame oil. These ingredients come together to create a sweet and savory glaze with just the right amount of heat.

Here's how to make the Sweet and Spicy Soy Glaze:

Ingredients:

1/4 cup soy sauce
1/4 cup honey
2 cloves garlic, minced
1 tsp chili flakes
1 tbsp sesame oil

Instructions:

- In a small bowl, whisk together the soy sauce, honey, minced garlic, chili flakes, and sesame oil until well combined.
- Use a pastry brush to coat your pork cut of choice with the glaze, making sure to cover all sides.

- Place the pork on a baking sheet or in a baking dish, and bake or grill until cooked through, basting occasionally with additional glaze.
- Serve the pork hot, with any remaining glaze on the side for dipping.
- One of the things I love about this glaze is how easy it is to customize. If you like your glaze sweeter, you can add more honey, or if you like it spicier, you can add more chili flakes. You can also adjust the amounts of garlic and sesame oil to your liking.

This glaze is also perfect for meal prep, as you can make a big batch and store it in an airtight container in the fridge for up to a week. Simply brush the glaze onto your pork before cooking, and you'll have a delicious and flavorful meal in no time.

This Sweet and Spicy Soy Glaze is a must-try recipe for any pork lover looking to add some bold and delicious flavor to their meals. It's easy to make, customizable, and perfect for a variety of pork cuts and cooking methods.

Herb and Garlic Marinade

This marinade is made with a blend of fresh herbs, garlic, olive oil, and citrus juice, which combine to create a zesty and aromatic flavor profile. It works particularly well with pork chops, pork tenderloin, and pork loin roasts, and can be used for both grilling and roasting.

To make the marinade, start by finely chopping a combination of fresh herbs, such as rosemary, thyme, and parsley. Add the herbs to a large bowl along with minced garlic, olive oil, lemon or lime juice, salt, and black pepper. Whisk everything together until the ingredients are well combined.

To use the marinade, simply place your pork cut of choice in a large zip-top bag and pour the marinade over the top, making sure the pork is evenly coated. Seal the bag and refrigerate it for at least 30 minutes, or up to 24 hours for more flavor.

When you're ready to cook the pork, remove it from the marinade and discard any excess marinade. Grill or roast the pork according to your preferred method, being sure to cook it to a safe internal temperature of 145°F.

The Herb and Garlic Marinade is a versatile and delicious way to add flavor to pork, and it's also easy to customize to your tastes. Try experimenting with different combinations of herbs or adding a splash of balsamic vinegar for a tangy twist. You can also use the marinade for other meats or vegetables, making it a great addition to any home cook's repertoire.

One thing I love about this marinade is how well it pairs with other flavors and ingredients. For example, you can add a spoonful of Dijon mustard to the marinade for a tangy kick, or mix in some honey or brown sugar for a touch of sweetness.

Another great thing about this marinade is that it can be used for meal prep. You can marinate the pork in advance and store it in the refrigerator for up to 24 hours, making it a convenient option for busy weeknights or weekend gatherings.

In addition to its great flavor, this marinade also has some health benefits. The fresh herbs provide antioxidants, while garlic has been shown to have anti-inflammatory and immune-boosting properties.

The Herb and Garlic Marinade is a great addition to any home cook's repertoire. It's easy to make, versatile, and delicious, and it can transform a simple pork chop or tenderloin into a flavorful and satisfying meal. Whether you're grilling up some pork for a summer barbecue or roasting a tenderloin for a cozy winter dinner, this marinade is sure to impress.

Hoisin Glaze

This recipe is for a Hoisin Glaze, which is a sweet and savory sauce made with Hoisin sauce, soy sauce, garlic, honey, and other seasonings.

To make this glaze, start by whisking together 1/2 cup of Hoisin sauce, 1/4 cup of soy sauce, 1 tablespoon of honey, 1 tablespoon of rice vinegar, 1 teaspoon of minced garlic, and 1 teaspoon of grated ginger in a small bowl. Once everything is combined, you can use the glaze to coat pork chops, pork tenderloin, or any other pork cut you like.

To use the Hoisin Glaze, first prepare your pork as desired. You can season it with salt and pepper, or marinate it in other seasonings if you prefer. Then, brush a generous amount of the Hoisin Glaze onto the pork, making sure to cover all sides. You can also reserve some of the glaze for basting the pork as it cooks.

Once your pork is coated with the Hoisin Glaze, you can cook it according to your preferred method. For example, you can grill or bake the pork until it's cooked through and the glaze has caramelized on the surface. Alternatively, you can pan-fry or broil the pork until it's crispy and caramelized on the outside, but still tender and juicy on the inside.

The result is a delicious and flavorful pork dish with a sweet and savory glaze that complements the natural flavors of the meat. The Hoisin Glaze can also be used in a variety of other dishes, such as stir-fry, noodles, or as a dipping sauce for spring rolls or other appetizers.

The Hoisin Glaze is a versatile and delicious addition to any pork recipe, adding a unique and flavorful twist to your favorite pork dishes. Whether you're cooking for a weeknight dinner or a special occasion, this glaze is sure to impress your guests and make your meal memorable.

CHAPTER 6

Desserts

In this section, I've included a variety of sweet and savory dessert recipes that are sure to surprise and delight your taste buds.

First up, we have Bacon and Bourbon Brownies, a decadent and indulgent dessert that combines rich chocolate, crispy bacon, and smooth bourbon. To make this recipe, you'll need to start by cooking the bacon until crispy, then chop it up and add it to the brownie batter along with a splash of bourbon. The result is a rich and fudgy brownie with a hint of smoky bacon and warm bourbon.

Next, we have Maple-Bacon Popcorn Balls, a playful and fun dessert that's perfect for sharing. To make this recipe, you'll need to pop some popcorn, then mix it with melted butter, maple syrup, and crispy bacon pieces before shaping it into balls. This sweet and salty treat is a crowd-pleaser that's perfect for game night or movie night at home.

For something a little more savory, try the Pork and Apple Hand Pies. These hand-held pies are filled with tender pork, sweet apples, and warm spices, all wrapped up in a flaky pastry crust. To make this recipe, you'll need to cook the pork and apple filling on the stove, then cut the pastry dough into rounds and fill them with the mixture before baking until golden brown.

We have Candied Bacon Bites, a simple and addictive dessert that's perfect for a sweet and salty snack. To make this recipe, you'll need to coat bacon slices in brown sugar and bake them until crispy and caramelized. The result is a crunchy and sweet bite that's perfect for serving as a snack or dessert.

These pork-based desserts are a unique and unexpected way to incorporate pork into your sweet treats. Whether you're in the mood for something indulgent like the Bacon and Bourbon Brownies, or something playful like the Maple-Bacon Popcorn Balls, there's a recipe in this cookbook to satisfy every sweet tooth.

Maple Bacon Cupcakes

To make these delicious cupcakes, you'll start by baking a batch of your favorite vanilla cupcakes. While they're cooling, you can prepare the maple bacon topping. To make the topping, you'll need crispy bacon, maple syrup, and a little bit of brown sugar. Simply cook the bacon until it's crispy, then chop it up into small pieces and mix it with the maple syrup and brown sugar.

Once your cupcakes have cooled, you can frost them with a simple cream cheese frosting. I like to add a little bit of maple syrup to the frosting for extra flavor, but you can adjust the sweetness to your liking.

Finally, it's time to assemble the cupcakes. Take a spoonful of the maple bacon topping and spoon it onto each cupcake, then gently press it down so it sticks to the frosting. You can sprinkle a little extra bacon on top for added crunch and flavor.

The result is a delicious and unexpected treat that's sure to impress your friends and family. The sweetness of the vanilla cupcakes and cream cheese frosting pairs perfectly with the salty, smoky flavor of the bacon and the sweetness of the maple syrup. These cupcakes are great for special occasions or just as a fun weekend baking project.

The Maple Bacon Cupcakes are a unique and delicious addition to the "Easy and Delicious Pork Recipes" cookbook. They're easy to make, but impressive to serve, and are sure to become a new favorite among readers.

Brown Sugar Pork Belly Bites with Cinnamon Cream Cheese Dip

I'm excited to share my recipe for Brown Sugar Pork Belly Bites with Cinnamon Cream Cheese Dip.

To start, you'll need to gather the ingredients for the pork belly bites. You'll need pork belly, brown sugar, soy sauce, garlic, and a few other spices to create a sweet and savory marinade. Once the pork belly is marinated, it's baked in the oven until it's tender and caramelized.

While the pork belly bites are cooking, you can prepare the cinnamon cream cheese dip. This dip features cream cheese, powdered sugar, vanilla extract, and ground cinnamon, which come together to create a sweet and tangy dip that pairs perfectly with the pork belly bites.

To serve, simply arrange the pork belly bites on a platter and serve with the cinnamon cream cheese dip on the side. Your guests will love the combination of sweet and savory flavors in this delicious appetizer.

What I love about this recipe is that it's easy to prepare and can be made ahead of time, making it perfect for entertaining. The pork belly bites are incredibly flavorful and tender, with a delicious caramelized crust that's sure to impress. And the cinnamon cream cheese dip adds a perfect touch of sweetness and tanginess to the dish.

Brown Sugar Pork Belly Bites with Cinnamon Cream Cheese Dip is a fun and flavorful recipe that's perfect for any occasion. Whether you're hosting a party or just looking for a delicious snack to share with friends, this recipe is sure to be a hit.

Spiced Apple and Pork Hand Pies

In this section of the book, I've included my recipe for Spiced Apple and Pork Hand Pies, a flavorful and easy-to-make dish that's perfect for a quick lunch or snack.

To start, you'll need to prepare the filling for the hand pies. I recommend using a combination of ground pork, apples, onion, and spices to create a sweet and savory filling that's packed with flavor. Start by browning the ground pork in a skillet, then add diced apples and onions to the pan and sauté until they're tender. Add a mixture of spices, including cinnamon, nutmeg, and cloves, to give the filling a warm and spicy flavor.

Once the filling is prepared, it's time to assemble the hand pies. I recommend using pre-made pie dough, which can be found in most grocery stores. Cut the dough into small circles using a cookie cutter, then place a spoonful of the filling in the center of each circle. Fold the dough over the filling, then press the edges together to seal the pies. Brush the tops of the pies with an egg wash, then bake in the oven until they're golden brown and crispy.

The result is a delicious and portable hand pie that's perfect for a quick lunch or snack on the go. The combination of sweet apples and savory pork is perfectly balanced, while the spices add warmth and depth of flavor. These hand pies can be enjoyed warm or cold, making them a versatile option for any time of day.

The Spiced Apple and Pork Hand Pies recipe is a great addition to any pork lover's recipe collection. It's easy to make, flavorful, and perfect for enjoying on the go. With this recipe and others like it, readers will be able to discover new and delicious ways to enjoy pork in all its forms.

Pork Rind Churros with Chocolate Dipping Sauce

To make these churros, you'll need a few key ingredients, including pork rinds, almond flour, eggs, butter, cinnamon, and a few other pantry staples. The pork rinds add a crispy and flavorful texture to the churros, while the almond flour provides a gluten-free and low-carb alternative to traditional flour.

To start, you'll need to grind the pork rinds in a food processor until they are finely ground, then mix them with the almond flour, cinnamon, and other dry ingredients. In a separate bowl, beat the eggs and butter together until smooth, then gradually add the dry ingredients until you have a smooth and cohesive dough.

Next, you'll need to heat up some oil in a deep pot or skillet until it reaches 375 degrees Fahrenheit. Using a piping bag or a churro maker, pipe the dough into long, thin strips and carefully lower them into the hot oil. Cook the churros until they are golden brown and crispy, then remove them from the oil and place them on a paper towel-lined plate to cool.

For the chocolate dipping sauce, you'll need some high-quality chocolate chips, heavy cream, and a pinch of salt. Simply melt the chocolate chips and cream together in a double boiler or in the microwave, then stir in the salt until smooth and silky.

To serve the churros, sprinkle them with a little bit of cinnamon sugar and serve them alongside the chocolate dipping sauce. The combination of the crispy and flavorful pork rind churros with the rich and decadent chocolate dipping sauce is sure to be a crowd-pleaser.

Pork Rind Churros with Chocolate Dipping Sauce is a fun and unique recipe that's perfect for a special occasion or as a special treat. With its unique combination of flavors and textures, this recipe is sure to be a hit with anyone who tries it.

CHAPTER 7

Cooking Tips and Techniques

In this section, I'll cover everything from choosing the right cuts of pork to the best cooking methods and temperature guidelines.

Choosing Cuts of Pork:
One of the most important factors in cooking pork is selecting the right cuts. Different cuts of pork have varying levels of fat, connective tissue, and tenderness, which means they require different cooking methods to achieve optimal flavor and texture. Some popular cuts of pork include pork tenderloin, pork chops, pork shoulder, and pork belly. When selecting cuts of pork, look for meat that is firm, moist, and has a bright pink color. Avoid meat that is discolored or has a strong odor.

Trimming and Seasoning Pork:
Before cooking pork, it's important to trim away any excess fat or connective tissue to ensure even cooking and a more tender finished product. Depending on the recipe, you may also want to season the pork with herbs, spices, or marinades to add flavor. When seasoning pork, be sure to use enough seasoning to coat the meat evenly, but don't go overboard or it may become too salty or overpowering.

Cooking Methods for Pork:
Pork can be cooked using a variety of methods, including grilling, roasting, slow-cooking, and pan-frying. The best method depends on the cut of pork and the desired end result. For example, a lean cut like pork tenderloin is best cooked quickly at high heat, while a tougher cut like pork shoulder is best slow-cooked to break down the connective tissue and create a tender finished product. When selecting a cooking method, consider the cut of pork, the amount of time you have available, and the equipment you have on hand.

Temperature Guidelines for Pork:
One of the most important factors in cooking pork is ensuring it reaches a safe internal temperature to avoid the risk of foodborne illness. The USDA recommends cooking pork to an internal temperature of 145°F (63°C) for medium-rare and 160°F (71°C) for medium. Ground pork should be cooked to an internal temperature of 160°F (71°C). To check the temperature of pork, use a meat thermometer inserted into the thickest part of the meat.

Resting Pork:
After cooking pork, it's important to let it rest for a few minutes before slicing or serving. This allows the juices to redistribute throughout the meat, resulting in a more tender and flavorful finished product. To rest pork, simply remove it from the heat source and let it sit for 5-10 minutes before slicing or serving.

By following these cooking tips and techniques, you'll be able to select, prepare, and cook pork with confidence and achieve delicious and satisfying results every time. Remember to select the right cuts of pork, trim and season the meat properly, choose the best cooking method for the cut, and use a meat thermometer to check for doneness. With a little practice and experimentation, you'll soon be whipping up delicious pork dishes that will impress your family and friends.

Properly Trimming and Seasoning Pork Cuts

When it comes to trimming pork cuts, it's important to remove any excess fat and silver skin. Fat can add flavor and juiciness to pork, but too much fat can make it greasy and unappetizing. Silver skin is a tough, fibrous layer of connective tissue that can make pork chewy and difficult to eat. To trim pork cuts, start by using a sharp knife to remove any large pieces of fat or silver skin, then trim away any remaining smaller pieces as needed.

Once you've trimmed your pork cuts, it's time to season them. The key to properly seasoning pork is to balance flavors and enhance the natural taste of the meat. Salt is a crucial component of any good pork seasoning, as it helps to tenderize the meat and enhance its flavor. Other common pork seasonings include black pepper, garlic powder, onion powder, paprika, and herbs like thyme and rosemary.

When seasoning pork, it's important to be mindful of the cut and cooking method. For example, if you're grilling pork chops, you may want to use a simple seasoning blend of salt, pepper, and garlic powder to let the natural flavor of the meat shine through. If you're slow-cooking a pork shoulder for pulled pork, you may want to use a more complex seasoning blend with paprika, cumin, and chili powder for a smoky and flavorful result.

One important tip for seasoning pork is to always taste as you go. Start with a small amount of seasoning and add more as needed, tasting the meat frequently to ensure it's not too salty or overpowering. Remember that seasoning is a personal preference, so feel free to adjust the amounts and types of seasonings to suit your taste.

Properly trimming and seasoning pork cuts is an essential step in creating delicious and flavorful pork dishes. By following these tips and techniques, you'll be able to prepare pork cuts that are tender, juicy, and bursting with flavor.

Choosing the Right Cooking Method

This is an important consideration when cooking pork, as different cuts of meat require different cooking techniques to achieve the best flavor and texture.

One important factor to consider when choosing a cooking method for pork is the cut of meat itself. For example, leaner cuts of pork, such as pork tenderloin or loin chops, are best cooked quickly over high heat, such as grilling or pan-searing. This helps to maintain their tenderness and juiciness, as overcooking can result in tough and dry meat.

On the other hand, tougher cuts of pork, such as pork shoulder or pork belly, require slow cooking methods to break down the connective tissue and create tender, flavorful meat. This can include methods like braising, slow-roasting, or cooking in a slow cooker.

Another important factor to consider when choosing a cooking method for pork is the flavor profile you want to achieve. For example, if you're looking for a smoky, charred flavor, grilling or smoking pork is a great choice. If you want a crisp, golden exterior, pan-frying or roasting can achieve that.

Additionally, certain cooking methods are better suited for specific types of recipes. For example, pork chops or tenderloin are great for stir-fry dishes or salads, while pork shoulder is ideal for making pulled pork or carnitas.

Ultimately, the key to choosing the right cooking method for pork is to understand the characteristics of the cut of meat you're working with, and to choose a cooking technique that will enhance its flavor and texture. Experimenting with different cooking methods can also be a fun and rewarding way to discover new ways to enjoy pork.

In this cookbook, I have included detailed instructions and cooking tips for each recipe, including recommended cooking methods for each cut of pork. This way, readers can feel confident in selecting the right cooking method for each recipe, and can explore new and delicious ways to enjoy this versatile and flavorful meat.

Here are some additional tips to help you choose the right cooking method for different cuts of pork:

Consider the thickness and size of the meat: Thin cuts of pork, such as pork chops, are best cooked quickly over high heat, while thicker cuts, such as pork loin or pork shoulder, benefit from slow-cooking methods.

Think about the desired texture: If you want tender and juicy pork, you may want to choose a cooking method that involves slow-cooking or braising, while if you want a crispy exterior and a juicy interior, a method like roasting or grilling can be a good choice.

Consider the level of doneness: Different cuts of pork have different recommended internal temperatures for safe consumption. For example, pork tenderloin should be cooked to an internal temperature of 145°F, while ground pork should be cooked to 160°F. Make sure to use a meat thermometer to ensure that the pork is cooked to the appropriate temperature.

Think about the flavors and seasonings you want to incorporate: Different cooking methods can help bring out different flavors in pork. For example, smoking or grilling can create a smoky flavor, while slow-cooking or braising can help to infuse the meat with flavorful sauces and spices.

Consider the equipment you have available: Some cooking methods require specific equipment, such as a slow cooker or a grill. Make sure to choose a cooking method that you have the appropriate equipment for.

By considering these factors when selecting a cooking method for pork, you can create delicious and flavorful dishes that showcase the unique qualities of each cut of meat. The cookbook includes a variety of recipes that utilize different cooking methods, so readers can experiment with different techniques and find their favorite ways to cook pork.

Tips for Grilling, Roasting, Slow-cooking and Frying

I'll share some tips and techniques for grilling, roasting, slow-cooking, and frying pork, to help readers feel confident in selecting and preparing different cuts of pork for different recipes.

Grilling:
Grilling is a popular cooking method for pork, especially for tender cuts like pork chops, tenderloin, and ribs. To achieve the best results, start by preheating your grill to medium-high heat and oiling the grates to prevent sticking. Then, season your pork with a dry rub or marinade, and place it on the grill, cooking it for about 5-6 minutes per side, or until the internal temperature reaches 145°F. Remember to let your pork rest for a few minutes before slicing it to allow the juices to redistribute.

Roasting:
Roasting is a great cooking method for larger cuts of pork, like pork loin or shoulder. To roast pork, preheat your oven to 350°F, season your pork with salt, pepper, and any other desired herbs or spices, and place it in a roasting pan. Roast the pork for about 20-25 minutes per pound, or until the internal temperature reaches 145°F. To keep the pork moist, baste it occasionally with

the pan drippings, and let it rest for about 10-15 minutes before slicing.

Slow-Cooking:
Slow-cooking is an excellent cooking method for tough cuts of pork, like pork shoulder or butt, that benefit from low and slow cooking to break down the collagen and become tender. To slow-cook pork, season it with a dry rub or marinade, and place it in a slow cooker with some liquid, like broth or barbecue sauce. Cook on low heat for 6-8 hours, or until the pork is tender and falls apart easily. For crispy edges, transfer the pork to a baking sheet and broil for a few minutes before serving.

Frying:
Frying is a quick and easy cooking method for pork, perfect for cutlets or strips that cook quickly. To fry pork, heat oil in a skillet over medium-high heat, and dredge the pork in seasoned flour or breadcrumbs. Fry the pork for about 3-4 minutes per side, or until golden brown and crispy. To avoid overcooking or drying out the pork, use a meat thermometer to check the internal temperature, which should reach 145°F.

Choosing the right cooking method for pork can make all the difference in achieving the best flavor and texture. By following these tips and techniques for grilling, roasting, slow-cooking, and frying pork, readers can feel confident in preparing delicious and easy pork recipes in a variety of styles.

Temperature Guidelines for Cooking Pork

Pork can be cooked in a variety of ways, from grilling and roasting to slow-cooking and pan-frying, and the cooking time and temperature can vary depending on the cut of pork and the cooking method used.

To ensure that pork is safe to eat, it's important to cook it to a minimum internal temperature of 145°F (63°C), as recommended by the USDA. This temperature applies to all cuts of pork, including ground pork, and should be measured with a meat thermometer inserted into the thickest part of the meat.

Here are some general guidelines for cooking pork to a safe internal temperature:

Pork chops and tenderloin: For pork chops and tenderloin, I recommend cooking to an internal temperature of 145°F (63°C). This can be achieved by grilling, roasting, or pan-frying the pork for 6-8 minutes per side, depending on the thickness of the meat.

Pork shoulder and butt: For larger cuts of pork such as shoulder and butt, I recommend slow-cooking the meat for several hours until it reaches an internal temperature of 195°F (90°C) or higher. This will ensure that the meat is tender and fully cooked through.

Pork ribs: Pork ribs can be cooked in a variety of ways, including grilling, smoking, or slow-cooking. To ensure that the ribs are fully cooked and tender, I recommend cooking them to an internal temperature of 190°F (88°C).

Ground pork: Ground pork should always be cooked to an internal temperature of 160°F (71°C) to ensure that any harmful bacteria are killed. This can be achieved by cooking ground pork in a skillet or on the grill until it's browned and fully cooked through.

By following these temperature guidelines and using a meat thermometer to ensure that pork is fully cooked, readers can enjoy safe and delicious pork dishes every time. It's also important to remember that letting cooked pork rest for a few minutes before slicing or serving can help to ensure that the meat is juicy and tender.
In addition to cooking pork to a safe internal temperature, there are a few other tips and tricks to keep in mind when cooking pork to ensure optimal flavor and texture. Here are a few of my favorite tips:

Bring pork to room temperature before cooking: To ensure that pork cooks evenly, it's a good idea to let it come to room temperature before cooking. This can take anywhere from 30 minutes to an hour, depending on the size of the meat.

Season generously: Pork is a versatile meat that can be flavored in a variety of ways. I recommend seasoning pork with a generous amount of salt and pepper, as well as any other herbs, spices, or marinades that you prefer.

Don't overcook: While it's important to cook pork to a safe internal temperature, it's also important not to overcook it. Overcooked pork can become tough and dry. Use a meat thermometer to ensure that the pork is fully cooked but still juicy and tender.

Let cooked pork rest: After cooking pork, it's a good idea to let it rest for a few minutes before slicing or serving. This allows the juices to redistribute throughout the meat, resulting in a juicier and more flavorful dish.

By following these guidelines and tips, readers of the cookbook "Easy and Delicious Pork Recipes" can enjoy a wide variety of pork dishes that are both safe and delicious. Whether grilling pork chops, slow-cooking pork shoulder, or pan-frying ground pork, these tips and temperature guidelines will help ensure that every pork dish turns out perfectly.

CHAPTER 8

Regional Pork Recipes

First up, we have Southern-style Pulled Pork with Vinegar Sauce, a classic recipe that's perfect for summer barbecues and family gatherings. This recipe features a pork shoulder that's slow-cooked until it falls apart, then tossed in a tangy vinegar-based sauce that's both sweet and savory. I recommend serving this pulled pork on soft buns with coleslaw and pickles for the ultimate Southern-style sandwich.

Next, we have Cuban-style Pork Shoulder with Mojo Sauce, a flavorful and aromatic recipe that's perfect for a festive dinner party. This recipe features a pork shoulder that's marinated in a garlic and citrus-based mojo sauce for several hours, then roasted until crispy and tender. I recommend serving this pork with black beans, rice, and some fresh avocado slices for a delicious and satisfying meal.

For something a little more exotic, try the Chinese-style Char Siu Pork, a sweet and savory dish that's a favorite in Chinese cuisine. This recipe features pork loin that's marinated in a blend of soy sauce, honey, and Chinese five-spice powder, then roasted until caramelized and delicious. I recommend serving this pork with steamed rice and some stir-fried vegetables for a complete and satisfying meal.

Another classic pork recipe from Germany is Pork Schnitzel, a breaded and pan-fried pork cutlet that's a staple of German cuisine. This recipe features pork cutlets that are pounded thin, coated in breadcrumbs, and pan-fried until crispy and golden. I recommend serving this schnitzel with some spaetzle or mashed potatoes and some tangy sauerkraut for a delicious and hearty meal.

Finally, we have Mexican-style Pork Tamales, a traditional recipe that's perfect for a festive occasion or special family dinner. This recipe features pork shoulder that's slow-cooked in a spicy tomato sauce until it's fall-apart tender, then wrapped in masa dough and steamed until cooked through. I recommend serving these tamales with some fresh pico de gallo and some guacamole for a complete and satisfying meal.

These regional pork recipes are a delicious way to experience different cultures and cuisines from around the world. Whether you're in the mood for the tangy and sweet flavors of Southern-style Pulled Pork or the exotic spices of Chinese-style Char Siu Pork, there's a recipe in this cookbook to suit every taste and occasion.

By featuring recipes from different regions, readers can experience new flavors and learn about different cooking techniques, while also adding some variety to their pork dishes.

In addition to the recipes mentioned above, I've included other regional pork recipes such as Spanish-style Pork with Chorizo and Potatoes, Italian-style Pork Ragu, Thai-style Pork Stir Fry, and many more. Each recipe is carefully crafted to bring out the unique flavors and textures of the region it represents.

For example, the Spanish-style Pork with Chorizo and Potatoes is a hearty and warming dish that's perfect for a cold winter evening. This recipe features pork shoulder that's slow-cooked with spicy chorizo sausage and potatoes, then seasoned with smoked paprika and other traditional Spanish spices. The result is a dish that's full of rich and bold flavors, and perfect for serving with crusty bread to soak up all the delicious juices.

On the other hand, the Italian-style Pork Ragu is a comforting and delicious recipe that's perfect for a Sunday family dinner. This recipe features pork shoulder that's slow-cooked with tomatoes, garlic, and herbs, then served over pasta for a classic Italian dish. The slow-cooking process allows the pork to become tender and flavorful, while the tomato sauce adds a sweet and savory element to the dish.

The Thai-style Pork Stir Fry is a flavorful and healthy recipe that's perfect for a quick weeknight dinner. This recipe features tender slices of pork loin that are stir-fried with colorful vegetables and a spicy, tangy sauce made with soy sauce, chili paste, and lime juice. The result is a dish that's both satisfying and delicious, and perfect for serving with steamed rice or noodles.

The regional pork recipes in this cookbook offer a diverse and exciting range of flavors and cooking styles that are sure to delight any pork lover. Whether you're in the mood for something hearty and warming like the Spanish-style Pork with Chorizo and Potatoes, or something light and refreshing like the Thai-style Pork Stir Fry, there's a recipe in this cookbook to suit every taste and occasion.

I also wanted to make sure that the regional pork recipes in this cookbook were accessible and easy to make for home cooks of all skill levels. Each recipe includes step-by-step instructions, as well as helpful tips and tricks for achieving the best results. Additionally, many of the ingredients used in these recipes can be found at most grocery stores or online, making it easy for readers to recreate these dishes in their own kitchens.

One of the key aspects of regional pork recipes is that they often use local ingredients and traditional cooking techniques. For example, the Spanish-style Pork with Chorizo and Potatoes uses smoked paprika, which is a staple in Spanish cuisine, and slow-cooking methods that are common in Spanish households. Similarly, the

Thai-style Pork Stir Fry uses traditional Thai ingredients like fish sauce and chili paste, and stir-frying techniques that are popular in Thai cuisine.

By including these regional pork recipes in this cookbook, I hope to inspire readers to try new flavors and cooking techniques, and to appreciate the rich and diverse culinary traditions found across the world. Whether you're looking for a classic Southern-style Pulled Pork recipe, or a more exotic Chinese-style Char Siu Pork recipe, there's something in this cookbook for everyone to enjoy.

The pork recipes in this book are designed to showcase the diverse flavors and cooking styles of different cultures around the world. Each recipe is accessible and easy to make, while also incorporating traditional ingredients and cooking techniques from the region it represents. I hope that readers will enjoy exploring these recipes, and discover new and exciting ways to cook with pork.

Southern-style Pulled Pork with Vinegar Sauce

This recipe is a true crowd-pleaser, with tender and juicy pulled pork that's slow-cooked until it falls apart, and a tangy and flavorful vinegar sauce that's the perfect complement to the pork.

To start, you'll need a pork shoulder or butt, which is a tough and flavorful cut that's perfect for slow cooking. I recommend using a bone-in pork shoulder for maximum flavor, but you can also use a boneless pork shoulder if that's what you have on hand. To prepare the pork, you'll need to season it generously with a spice rub that includes paprika, garlic powder, onion powder, salt, and pepper. Rub the spices all over the pork, then refrigerate it for at least 2 hours or overnight to let the flavors meld.

When you're ready to cook the pork, preheat your oven to 225°F. Place the pork in a large roasting pan and cover it tightly with foil. Roast the pork for 8-10 hours, or until it's very tender and falling apart. You can also cook the pork in a slow cooker on low for 8-10 hours, if you prefer.

While the pork is cooking, it's time to prepare the vinegar sauce. In a small saucepan, combine apple cider vinegar, brown sugar, ketchup, Worcestershire sauce, red pepper flakes, and salt. Bring the sauce to a simmer over medium heat, then reduce the heat to low and let it simmer for 10-15 minutes, or until it's thick and flavorful.

Once the pork is cooked, remove it from the oven or slow cooker and let it cool slightly. Use two forks to shred the pork into small pieces, discarding any large pieces of fat or bone. Pour the vinegar sauce over the pulled pork and toss to coat evenly.

To serve, you can pile the pulled pork onto buns and serve with coleslaw for a classic pulled pork sandwich, or serve it over rice or grits for a hearty and delicious meal. This Southern-style pulled pork with vinegar sauce is a true crowd-pleaser that's perfect for any occasion, from backyard barbecues to weeknight dinners.

If you're looking to add some extra flavor and heat to your pulled pork, you can also add a few dashes of hot sauce or cayenne pepper to the vinegar sauce. This will give your pulled pork a spicy kick that's sure to please anyone who loves bold flavors.

Another tip for making the perfect pulled pork is to let it rest for a few minutes after you've shredded it and tossed it with the vinegar sauce. This will allow the flavors to meld together and will make the pork even more tender and juicy.

If you have any leftover pulled pork, you can store it in an airtight container in the refrigerator for up to 3 days, or freeze it for later use. Leftover pulled pork is great for making sandwiches, tacos, quesadillas, or even pizza.

This Southern-style pulled pork with vinegar sauce is a delicious and satisfying recipe that's sure to become a new favorite in your household. With its tangy and flavorful sauce and tender, juicy pork, it's the perfect meal for any occasion, whether you're hosting a backyard barbecue or just looking for a hearty and delicious dinner.

Cuban-style Pork Shoulder with Mojo Sauce

The Cuban-style Pork Shoulder with Mojo Sauce is a perfect example of the delicious and vibrant flavors of Cuban cooking.

To start, you'll need a pork shoulder or butt roast, which will be marinated overnight in a flavorful mixture of orange juice, lime juice, garlic, oregano, and cumin. The next day, the pork is slow-roasted in the oven until it's tender and falling apart. The result is a juicy, flavorful roast that's perfect for shredding and serving in a variety of ways.

The real star of this recipe, though, is the Mojo sauce. This tangy and bright sauce is made with garlic, olive oil, citrus juice, and a touch of vinegar, and it's the perfect accompaniment to the rich and savory pork. To make the Mojo sauce, you'll simply whisk together the ingredients and let it sit for a bit to allow the flavors to meld.

To serve the pork, you can either shred it and serve it with the Mojo sauce on the side, or you can spoon the sauce over the pork and let it soak in. This dish is traditionally served with rice and black beans, but you could also serve it with roasted vegetables, plantains, or a fresh salad.

The Cuban-style Pork Shoulder with Mojo Sauce is a delicious and easy-to-make recipe that's sure to impress. The marinade and Mojo sauce infuse the pork with bright and bold flavors, making it a perfect centerpiece for a Cuban-inspired feast. This dish is also great for meal prep, as you can use the leftovers in tacos, burritos, or sandwiches throughout the week.

If you're short on time, you could also try making this recipe in a slow cooker or Instant Pot. Simply brown the pork shoulder first, then transfer it to your slow cooker or Instant Pot with the marinade and cook on low for 8-10 hours or on high for 4-6 hours. The result will be the same tender and flavorful pork that's perfect for shredding and serving with the Mojo sauce.

One thing to keep in mind with this recipe is that the marinade and Mojo sauce both contain a fair amount of acid from the citrus juices. While this gives the dish its bright and tangy flavor, it can also cause the pork to become a bit tough if it's overcooked or left in the marinade for too long. For best results, be sure to follow the recommended cooking times and allow the pork to rest for a few minutes before slicing or shredding.

In addition to its delicious flavor, the Cuban-style Pork Shoulder with Mojo Sauce is also a great source of protein and healthy fats. Pork shoulder is a relatively affordable cut of meat, and it's packed with protein, vitamins, and minerals. The Mojo sauce is also a great source of healthy fats from the olive oil, which can help keep you feeling satisfied and full.

Overall, the Cuban-style Pork Shoulder with Mojo Sauce is a must-try recipe for anyone who loves bold and flavorful cuisine. Whether you're looking to add some variety to your meal prep routine or impress guests with a delicious and easy-to-make main dish, this recipe is sure to become a new favorite.

Chinese-style Char Siu Pork

Char Siu Pork is a popular Cantonese dish that's often found in Chinese BBQ restaurants, and it's known for its succulent and flavorful pork that's been marinated and roasted until tender.

To make this recipe, you'll need to start by marinating pork tenderloin in a flavorful mixture of soy sauce, honey, hoisin sauce, and a few key spices. I like to marinate the pork overnight for maximum flavor, but you can also marinate it for a few hours if you're short on time.

Once the pork is marinated, it's time to roast it in the oven or on the grill. I recommend roasting the pork in a hot oven (around 400°F) for 15-20 minutes, or until the internal temperature reaches 145°F. You can also grill the pork over high heat, turning it occasionally until it's nicely browned and cooked through.

While the pork is roasting, you can prepare the glaze by combining more soy sauce, honey, and hoisin sauce with a bit of rice vinegar and sesame oil. Once the pork is cooked through, brush it with the glaze and return it to the oven or grill for a few minutes to allow the glaze to caramelize and create a nice crust on the outside of the pork.

To serve the Char Siu Pork, I like to slice it thinly and serve it over rice with some steamed vegetables and a sprinkle of green onions. You can also use the pork in stir-fries or noodles dishes for a delicious and flavorful twist.

Chinese-style Char Siu Pork recipe is a great way to add some international flavor to your dinner table, and it's surprisingly easy to make at home. With a few simple ingredients and some basic cooking techniques, you can enjoy this delicious and flavorful pork dish any night of the week.

For those who are interested in exploring the flavors of Chinese cuisine, this Char Siu Pork recipe is a great place to start. The combination of sweet and savory flavors, along with the tender and juicy pork, makes for a truly delicious and satisfying meal.

One of the great things about this recipe is that it's very versatile. You can adjust the level of sweetness or spice to suit your preferences, and you can also experiment with different cuts of pork or even try it with chicken or beef.

To take this recipe to the next level, you can also try adding some additional flavors to the marinade or glaze. For example, you could add some five-spice powder or garlic to the marinade for an extra kick of flavor. Or, you could add some chili paste or sriracha to the glaze for a spicy twist.

This Chinese-style Char Siu Pork recipe is a delicious and easy way to explore the flavors of Chinese cuisine. Whether you're cooking for a crowd or just want to enjoy a flavorful meal at home, this recipe is sure to become a new favorite.

German-style Pork Schnitzel

This classic dish is a staple in German cuisine and is loved for its crispy texture and savory flavor. It's also surprisingly easy to make at home with just a few simple ingredients.

To make my German-style Pork Schnitzel recipe, you'll need the following ingredients:

4 boneless pork chops, pounded to an even thickness
1 cup all-purpose flour
2 eggs, beaten
1 cup breadcrumbs
1 tsp salt
1 tsp black pepper
1 tsp paprika
1/2 tsp garlic powder
1/2 cup vegetable oil, for frying
Lemon wedges, for serving
To begin, set up a breading station with three shallow bowls. In the first bowl, add the flour. In the second bowl, whisk together the eggs. In the third bowl, combine the breadcrumbs, salt, pepper, paprika, and garlic powder.

Next, season the pork chops with salt and pepper. Dredge each pork chop in the flour, shaking off any excess. Dip the floured pork chop into the beaten egg, then coat it in the breadcrumb mixture. Press the breadcrumbs onto the pork chop to make sure they stick.

In a large skillet, heat the vegetable oil over medium-high heat until hot. Add the breaded pork chops to the skillet and cook for 3-4 minutes on each side, or until golden brown and crispy. Use a pair of tongs to flip the pork chops carefully, so the breading doesn't come off. Once cooked, remove the pork chops from the skillet and place them on a paper towel-lined plate to drain excess oil.

Serve the German-style Pork Schnitzel hot, with lemon wedges on the side for squeezing over the top. This dish pairs well with a side of mashed potatoes, sauerkraut, or a green salad.

This German-style Pork Schnitzel recipe is a delicious and easy-to-make dish that's perfect for a hearty weeknight meal or a festive dinner party. The crispy breading and savory pork flavor are sure to be a hit with everyone at the table. If you want to take this recipe to the next level, you can add some extra toppings to your German-style Pork Schnitzel.

Some classic toppings include a fried egg on top, a dollop of sour cream, or a slice of ham and cheese. These toppings can add even more flavor and richness to the dish.

You can switch up the seasonings in the breadcrumb mixture to add some variety to your Pork Schnitzel. For example, you can add some dried herbs like thyme or oregano, or swap out the paprika for some cayenne pepper for a spicy kick. You can also use panko breadcrumbs instead of regular breadcrumbs for an even crispier texture.

If you want to make this dish a bit healthier, you can also try baking the Pork Schnitzel instead of frying it. Simply preheat your oven to 400°F, place the breaded pork chops on a baking sheet lined with parchment paper, and bake for 20-25 minutes or until golden brown and cooked through. This method will result in a healthier version of the classic German-style Pork Schnitzel, while still maintaining its crispy texture and delicious flavor.

German-style Pork Schnitzel is a classic dish that's perfect for any pork lover. With a few simple ingredients and some basic cooking techniques, you can easily make this dish at home and impress your family and friends with your culinary skills.

Mexican-style Pork Tamales

This recipe is a classic, featuring tender and juicy pork filling wrapped in a flavorful masa dough and steamed until cooked through. Here's how to make it:

Ingredients:

2 lbs pork shoulder, cut into large chunks
1 onion, chopped
2 garlic cloves, minced
1 jalapeno pepper, chopped
1 tsp ground cumin
1 tsp chili powder
1 tsp paprika
Salt and pepper, to taste
2 cups masa harina
2 cups chicken broth
1 tsp baking powder
1/2 cup vegetable shortening
1/2 cup lard
Corn husks, soaked in warm water

Instructions:

- In a large pot, combine the pork shoulder, onion, garlic, jalapeno, cumin, chili powder, paprika, salt, and pepper. Cover with water and bring to a boil. Reduce the heat to low and simmer for 2-3 hours, or until the pork is tender and falls apart easily.

- Remove the pork from the pot and shred it using two forks. Reserve the cooking liquid.

- In a large mixing bowl, combine the masa harina, chicken broth, baking powder, shortening, and lard. Mix until a smooth dough forms.

To assemble the tamales, take a soaked corn husk and spread a thin layer of the masa dough on it, leaving a border around the edges. Spoon some of the pork filling onto the center of the masa dough.

Roll the tamale up tightly, tucking the edges of the corn husk in to seal it. Repeat with the remaining corn husks, masa dough, and pork filling.

Place the tamales in a steamer basket and set over a pot of boiling water. Cover and steam for 1-2 hours, or until the masa dough is cooked through.

Serve the tamales hot with your favorite toppings, such as salsa, sour cream, and chopped cilantro.

These Mexican-style Pork Tamales are a labor of love, but they're absolutely worth the effort. The tender and flavorful pork filling pairs perfectly with the slightly sweet and savory masa dough, creating a truly delicious and satisfying meal. Don't be intimidated by the process of making tamales – with a little patience and practice, you'll be a pro in no time. Here are a few tips to ensure your Mexican-style Pork Tamales turn out perfectly:

Soak the corn husks in warm water for at least 30 minutes before using them. This will make them pliable and easier to work with.

Don't overstuff your tamales. A little goes a long way with these, and you don't want to end up with filling spilling out of the sides.

If you're having trouble rolling your tamales, try using a piece of plastic wrap to help you. Simply place a piece of plastic wrap on your work surface, spread the masa dough over it, add your filling, and use the plastic wrap to roll everything up tightly.

Make sure your tamales are tightly wrapped before steaming them. You don't want any water getting inside and ruining the texture of the masa dough.

Don't be afraid to get creative with your toppings. While traditional toppings like salsa and sour cream are always delicious, you can also try adding things like queso fresco, diced avocado, or even pickled onions for a little extra flavor.

With these tips in mind, you'll be well on your way to making delicious and authentic Mexican-style Pork Tamales at home. And remember, practice makes perfect – the more you make them, the easier they'll become.

CHAPTER 9

Healthy Pork Recipes

First up, we have Grilled Pork Tenderloin with Mango Salsa, a light and refreshing meal that's perfect for warm weather. To make this recipe, I recommend marinating the pork tenderloin in a mixture of olive oil, lime juice, garlic, and spices, then grilling it until it's perfectly charred on the outside and juicy on the inside. Serve it with a fresh and flavorful mango salsa made with diced mango, red onion, cilantro, and lime juice.

Next, we have Pork and Bean Chili, a hearty and satisfying dish that's perfect for chilly evenings. This recipe features lean ground pork, kidney beans, and a variety of vegetables and spices for a healthy and flavorful chili that's packed with protein and fiber. I recommend using low-sodium broth and canned beans to keep the sodium content in check.

For a light and refreshing lunch option, try Vietnamese-style Pork and Rice Noodle Salad. This recipe combines grilled pork tenderloin with rice noodles, fresh herbs, and a tangy lime dressing for a delicious and healthy meal that's perfect for warm weather. To make this recipe, simply grill the pork tenderloin and toss it with cooked rice noodles, fresh herbs like mint and cilantro, and a tangy dressing made with lime juice, fish sauce, and honey.

For something a little heartier, try the Spicy Pork and Quinoa Bowl. This recipe features lean ground pork, quinoa, and a variety of vegetables and spices for a healthy and filling bowl that's perfect for meal prep or weeknight dinners. To make this recipe, simply brown the pork in a skillet with onion and garlic, then add cooked quinoa and a variety of veggies like bell peppers, corn, and black beans.

Overall, these healthy pork recipes are a delicious way to enjoy the nutritional benefits of pork while still maintaining a healthy and balanced diet. Whether you're in the mood for something light and refreshing like the Grilled Pork Tenderloin with Mango Salsa, or something hearty and satisfying like the Pork and Bean Chili, there's a recipe in this cookbook to suit every taste and dietary preference.

Another healthy pork recipe that I've included in this cookbook is Pork and Vegetable Stir-Fry. This recipe is a quick and easy way to get your daily serving of vegetables while still enjoying the flavor and nutrition of pork. To make this recipe, simply stir-fry thinly sliced pork loin with a variety of vegetables like broccoli, carrots, and bell peppers, then toss it all in a flavorful sauce made with soy sauce, ginger, and garlic.

For a unique and flavorful twist on traditional pork chops, try the Balsamic Glazed Pork Chops with Roasted Vegetables. This recipe features lean pork chops that are marinated in a mixture of balsamic vinegar, honey, and spices, then roasted in the oven until they're tender and juicy. Serve them with a side of roasted vegetables like sweet potatoes, Brussels sprouts, and carrots for a healthy and satisfying meal.

We have Slow-Cooker Pulled Pork Lettuce Wraps, a delicious and low-carb alternative to traditional pulled pork sandwiches. To make this recipe, simply slow-cook a pork shoulder with spices and broth until it's fall-apart tender, then serve it in lettuce cups with a variety of toppings like sliced avocado, cilantro, and diced tomatoes. This recipe is not only healthy and low-carb, but it's also a great way to use up leftover pork.

These healthy pork recipes are proof that you don't have to sacrifice flavor for nutrition. Whether you're in the mood for a light and refreshing salad or a hearty stir-fry, there's a recipe in this cookbook to suit your needs. By incorporating lean cuts of pork and a variety of vegetables and spices, you can enjoy delicious and nutritious meals that support your overall health and well-being.

Grilled Pork Tenderloin with Mango Salsa

To make this recipe, you'll need a pork tenderloin, some basic spices, and fresh ingredients for the mango salsa. Start by seasoning the pork tenderloin with salt, pepper, garlic powder, and paprika, then grill it over medium-high heat until it's cooked to your desired level of doneness. I recommend using a meat thermometer to ensure that the internal temperature of the pork reaches 145°F for optimal safety and flavor.

While the pork is grilling, you can prepare the mango salsa by combining diced mango, red onion, jalapeno, lime juice, and cilantro in a bowl. The salsa is the perfect complement to the savory pork, with its sweet and tangy flavor profile.

Once the pork tenderloin is done, let it rest for a few minutes before slicing it into medallions. Serve the pork with a generous spoonful of the mango salsa on top, and garnish with additional cilantro if desired.

One of the great things about this recipe is that it's versatile and can be customized to suit your tastes. For example, you could use a different type of fruit in the salsa, such as pineapple or peach, or adjust the spice level by adding more or less jalapeno. You could also experiment with different seasoning blends for the pork, such as a barbecue or Cajun rub.

The Grilled Pork Tenderloin with Mango Salsa recipe is a delicious and healthy option that's perfect for any occasion, from weeknight dinners to backyard barbecues. It's also a great way to showcase the versatility and flavor of pork, and to impress your family and friends with your culinary skills.

Another benefit of this recipe is that it's relatively easy to make, even for beginner cooks. Grilling the pork tenderloin is a simple and straightforward process, and the mango salsa comes together quickly with just a few ingredients. It's also a great way to incorporate more fresh fruits and vegetables into your diet, which can help boost your overall health and well-being.

If you're looking to elevate this recipe even further, you could serve the pork with a side of grilled or roasted vegetables, such as asparagus or sweet potatoes. You could also pair it with a refreshing summer salad or some crusty bread to soak up the delicious juices.

The Grilled Pork Tenderloin with Mango Salsa recipe is a fantastic addition to any cook's repertoire. It's healthy, flavorful, and easy to make, and can be customized to suit your tastes and preferences. Whether you're cooking for a crowd or just for yourself, this recipe is sure to impress and satisfy.

Pork and Bean Chili

This hearty and flavorful chili is perfect for cooler weather or when you're in the mood for something comforting and satisfying.

To make this recipe, you'll need the following

Ingredients:

2 lbs. pork shoulder, cut into small cubes
1 large onion, diced
3 cloves garlic, minced
1 green bell pepper, diced
1 can (15 oz.) kidney beans, drained and rinsed
1 can (15 oz.) black beans, drained and rinsed
1 can (15 oz.) tomato sauce
1 can (14.5 oz.) diced tomatoes, undrained
1 tablespoon chili powder
1 tablespoon ground cumin
1 teaspoon smoked paprika
1/2 teaspoon cayenne pepper
Salt and pepper, to taste

Sour cream, shredded cheese, and sliced green onions, for serving (optional)

To begin, heat a large Dutch oven or pot over medium-high heat. Add the pork cubes and cook until browned on all sides, stirring occasionally, about 5-7 minutes. Using a slotted spoon, transfer the pork to a plate and set aside.

In the same pot, add the onion, garlic, and bell pepper and sauté until softened, about 5 minutes. Add the chili powder, cumin, smoked paprika, and cayenne pepper, and stir to combine. Cook for another 1-2 minutes, or until fragrant.

Next, add the tomato sauce, diced tomatoes, and the browned pork cubes to the pot. Stir to combine, then bring the mixture to a simmer. Cover the pot with a lid and let the chili simmer for about 1-2 hours, or until the pork is tender and the flavors have melded together.

Once the pork is tender, add the kidney beans and black beans to the pot, and let them heat through, about 10 minutes. Season the chili with salt and pepper, to taste.

Serve the chili hot, garnished with a dollop of sour cream, shredded cheese, and sliced green onions, if desired.

This Pork and Bean Chili recipe is a crowd-pleaser and a great way to use up leftover pork shoulder. It's hearty, flavorful, and perfect for meal prep or a cozy night in. I hope you enjoy making and savoring this recipe as much as I do.

Vietnamese-style Pork and Rice Noodle Salad

Vietnamese-style Pork and Rice Noodle Salad. This recipe is inspired by the fresh and vibrant flavors of Vietnamese cuisine and is a perfect summer dish, with a refreshing mix of flavors and textures.

To make this recipe, you'll need to start by marinating thin slices of pork tenderloin in a mixture of fish sauce, sugar, garlic, and lime juice. While the pork marinates, you can prepare the other components of the dish, including rice noodles, thinly sliced vegetables like carrots and cucumbers, and fresh herbs like mint and cilantro.

Once everything is ready, it's time to assemble the salad. Start by laying a bed of rice noodles on a platter or individual plates, then add the sliced vegetables, fresh herbs, and sliced pork on top. Finish the dish with a drizzle of nuoc cham, a classic Vietnamese dipping sauce made with fish sauce, sugar, lime juice, and chili peppers.

What I love about this dish is that it's incredibly versatile - you can customize it to suit your preferences by adding or removing different ingredients. You could also try substituting the pork tenderloin for chicken or shrimp for a different twist on the recipe.

This Vietnamese-style Pork and Rice Noodle Salad is a light and refreshing dish that's perfect for a warm summer day or any time you're craving fresh and flavorful Vietnamese cuisine. With a combination of sweet, salty, and tangy flavors and a mix of textures, this salad is sure to become a new favorite in your recipe collection.

One of the great things about this recipe is that it's also very healthy, packed with protein from the pork tenderloin and fiber from the fresh vegetables. It's also gluten-free and can easily be made vegan by omitting the pork and using tofu or a plant-based protein instead.

Another benefit of this dish is that it's incredibly easy to prepare. While the pork tenderloin does need to marinate for at least 30 minutes, the actual cooking time is only a few minutes per side on the grill or in a grill pan. The rest of the ingredients can be prepped while the pork is marinating, making this a great option for a quick and easy weeknight meal.

I also love that this dish can be made in advance and stored in the refrigerator for a few days, making it a great option for meal prep or for entertaining. Simply store the cooked pork and vegetables separately from the rice noodles and herbs, then assemble the salad just before serving.

Vietnamese-style Pork and Rice Noodle Salad is a delicious and healthy option that's easy to prepare and incredibly versatile. Whether you're in the mood for a light and refreshing salad for lunch or a flavorful and satisfying dinner, this recipe is sure to hit the spot.

Pork and Veggie Skewers

To make the skewers, start by selecting your favorite vegetables, such as bell peppers, zucchini, cherry tomatoes, and red onions. Cut them into bite-sized pieces and set them aside while you prepare the pork.

For the pork, I recommend using pork loin, which is a lean and flavorful cut that's easy to work with. Cut the pork into bite-sized cubes and season it with a mixture of garlic, onion powder, smoked paprika, and a touch of honey for sweetness.

To assemble the skewers, alternate pieces of pork and veggies onto metal or wooden skewers, making sure to leave a little bit of space between each piece. If using wooden skewers, be sure to soak them in water for at least 30 minutes beforehand to prevent them from burning on the grill.

Once the skewers are assembled, it's time to cook them. You can either grill them over medium-high heat for about 10-12 minutes, turning occasionally, or broil them in the oven for about 10 minutes, flipping halfway through.

Once the skewers are cooked through and the veggies are tender, it's time to serve them up. I like to sprinkle a little bit of fresh parsley or cilantro on top for a pop of color and flavor, but you can also serve them as is or with your favorite dipping sauce.

Pork and Veggie Skewers are a delicious and healthy way to enjoy pork and a variety of fresh vegetables in one dish. With just a few simple ingredients and easy preparation, this recipe is a great option for busy weeknights or summer barbecues.

Another great thing about Pork and Veggie Skewers is that they are very customizable. You can switch up the veggies to suit your taste preferences or use whatever veggies you have on hand. For example, you can add mushrooms, eggplant, or even pineapple for a sweet and savory flavor.

If you want to add even more flavor to the skewers, you can marinate the pork before assembling the skewers. Simply mix together your favorite marinade ingredients, such as soy sauce, ginger, and garlic, and let the pork marinate in the mixture for at least an hour before assembling the skewers.

These skewers are also a great option for meal prep. You can assemble them ahead of time and store them in the refrigerator until you're ready to cook them. This is a great option if you're short on time during the week and want a quick and healthy meal.

In addition to being delicious and easy to make, Pork and Veggie Skewers are also a great source of protein and vitamins. The lean pork provides a good amount of protein while the vegetables provide fiber and important nutrients such as vitamin C and potassium.

Pork and Veggie Skewers are a versatile and healthy recipe that is sure to become a new favorite. With just a few simple ingredients and easy preparation, these skewers are perfect for busy weeknights or summer barbecues.

Spicy Pork and Quinoa Bowl

The Spicy Pork and Quinoa Bowl is a great option for those who want a satisfying and nutritious meal that's also packed with flavor.

To make this recipe, you'll need some basic ingredients such as pork tenderloin, quinoa, bell peppers, onions, and spices like cumin, chili powder, and paprika. You'll also need a few other ingredients like fresh lime juice, cilantro, and avocado to add some freshness and tanginess to the dish.

First, you'll want to cook the quinoa according to the package instructions, then set it aside while you prepare the rest of the ingredients. To cook the pork tenderloin, you can either grill it or cook it in a skillet until it's browned and cooked through. Once it's done, let it rest for a few minutes before slicing it into bite-sized pieces.

Next, you'll want to sauté the bell peppers and onions in the same skillet until they're tender and caramelized. Add in the spices and stir to coat the vegetables, then add the sliced pork and cook for another few minutes until everything is heated through and the flavors have melded together.

To assemble the bowl, start by spooning some cooked quinoa into a bowl, then top it with the pork and vegetable mixture. Garnish with fresh cilantro, sliced avocado, and a squeeze of lime juice for some brightness and tanginess.

The Spicy Pork and Quinoa Bowl is a delicious and healthy meal that's perfect for busy weeknights or meal prep. It's packed with protein, fiber, and essential vitamins and minerals, making it a great option for those who want to eat well without sacrificing flavor. And with its customizable toppings and seasonings, you can easily adjust this recipe to suit your own taste preferences.

For example, if you want to make the dish even spicier, you can add some extra chili powder or red pepper flakes. On the other hand, if you prefer a milder flavor, you can omit the spices altogether or reduce the amount used. You can also swap out the quinoa for brown rice or another grain of your choice, or add in some extra veggies like spinach or broccoli for some extra nutrition.

Another great thing about this recipe is that it's easy to make in large batches, so you can meal prep it for the week and have a delicious and healthy lunch or dinner ready to go whenever you need it. Simply cook up a big batch of quinoa and pork, then portion it out into containers with some fresh toppings and you're good to go.

Spicy Pork and Quinoa Bowl is a versatile and satisfying recipe that's perfect for anyone who wants to enjoy a healthy and flavorful meal without spending hours in the kitchen. Whether you're a busy professional or a health-conscious home cook, this recipe is sure to become a new favorite in your meal rotation.

Printed in Great Britain
by Amazon

33757237R00078